SOUTHERN COUNTIES
BIKE GUIDE

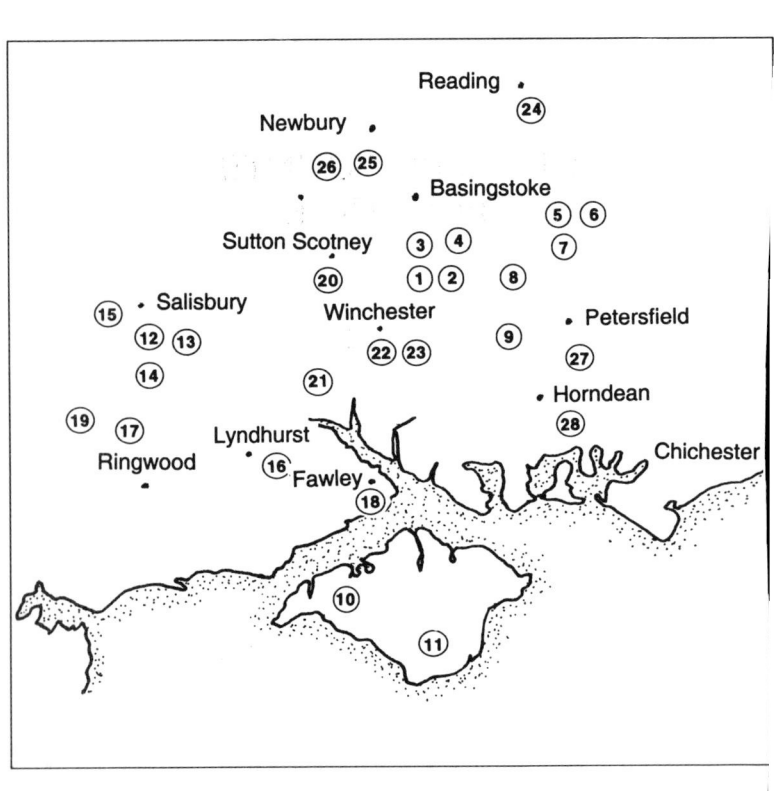

SOUTHERN COUNTIES BIKE GUIDE

(Hampshire, Berkshire, Wiltshire & West Sussex)

by

LILLIAN HOBBS

CICERONE PRESS
MILNTHORPE, CUMBRIA

© Lilian Hobbs 1994
ISBN 185284 163 X

A catalogue record for this book is available from the British Library

*To Mother
for
waiting patiently
in the car*

Front Cover: A junction of bridleways near Ventnor (Route 10)

Acknowledgements

This book would not be complete without a thank you to my colleagues at work, Iain Stephen and Ken England, who first introduced me to the mountain bike. Then of course there is my friend Iona McKenzie who accompanied me on many of these rides and never complained at the numerous stops made for note taking. Special thanks to Jeff Geary for scanning some of the maps on his computer. A big thank you for the help given by Jo Ronald and Andy Grattan-Kane in the Rights of Way Department of Hampshire County Council. To my local cycle shop, Peter Hansford Cycles in Chandlers Ford near Eastleigh, who took considerable time and trouble to ensure that I selected the right bike, and to Cyclerama in the Chandlers Ford Arcade for servicing my bike and to Raleigh and Claude Butler for making mountain bikes that have generated many happy hours.

Advice to Readers

Readers are advised that whilst every effort is taken by the author to ensure the accuracy of this guidebook, changes can occur which may affect the contents. It is advisable to check locally on transport, accommodation, shops etc but even rights of way can be altered, paths can be eradicated by landslip, forest fires or changes of ownership.

The publisher would welcome notes of any such changes.

Preface

This book is dedicated to mountain bike riders everywhere.

It is aimed at what I suspect is the typical mountain biker. An individual who works during the week, does not have, nor want to, train every night. However, at the weekend, he or she wants to take the mountain bike out for a ride: specifically for enjoyment but not to become too exhausted in the process! Therefore all the rides in this book will provide a challenge somewhere on the trail, and they can all be completed in less than an hour and fifteen minutes, consequently this does not disrupt the day too much.

This guide is intended to be a pocket reference of trails that can be followed. It should not be used as a substitute for a good OS map. The route sketches should be used as a guide only because they are not drawn to scale.

One very important point to remember is that you must not cycle on footpaths. Some of the trails may involve crossing a footpath. Please respect the law and the countryside code and dismount and push the bicycle. Some of the trails will involve going through gates. Please do not forget to close them behind you.

Since all these routes require a car to reach the starting point, please be considerate, careful and legal when selecting a place to park the car. Although I have tried to identify nearby car parks, it is not always possible and therefore be prepared to park the car in a nearby lay-by and cycle to the start of the ride. Please don't obstruct farm entrances.

Whilst every effort has been made to achieve accuracy in the production of the materials used in this guidebook. The author, publishers and copyright owners can accept no responsibility for: trespass, irresponsible riding, any loss or damage to persons or property suffered as a result of the route descriptions or advice offered in this book. The inclusion of a route in this guide does not in any way guarantee that the path or track involved is a right of way. Should a conflict with landowners occur, please dismount, leave by the shortest route possible and be polite with the people concerned. Subsequently the matter should be taken up with the local authority.

The author makes a plea to all landowners. Please post clearly, easily visible signs so that people do not unintentionally stray onto private land.

Contents

So You Own a Mountain Bike 9
Route Summary 12
Recommended Maps 13

North Winchester 15
   1.   Itchen Wood 15
   2.   Around Northington 17
   3.   Itchen Stoke Down 19
   4.   Abbotstone 22

Lasham 25
   5.   Closedown Wood 26
   6.   Weston Common - Long Lane Track 28
   7.   Weston Common 31

Alresford 34
   8.   Ox Drove 34
   9.   Four Marks 37

The Isle of Wight 42
   10.   Yarmouth 43
   11.   Ventnor 46

Salisbury 49
   12.   Clearbury Ring 50
   13.   Stratford Toney 52
   14.   Whitsbury Down 57
   15.   Knapp Down 60

New Forest 63
   16.   Ivy Wood Area 63
   17.   Ashley Heath 66
   18.   Lepe 68
   19.   Ringwood Forest 70

Winchester Area 73
   20. Sutton Scotney 73
   21. Compton Down 75

Cheesefoot Head 78
   22. Longwood Warren 78
   23. Fawley Down 80

Other Routes 84
   24. Along the A33 84
   25. Stubbington Down 87
   26. Watership Down 89
   27. Queen Elizabeth Forest 92
   28. Stansted Forest 95

Appendix 99
   Duration Report 99
   Distance Report 100
   Routes by Difficulty 102

So You Own a Mountain Bike

Congratulations, you have just bought a mountain bike and now you want to take it off road, but where do you go? Unless you already live in the country finding places to ride can be a major problem. What you have purchased is an expensive off-road vehicle, therefore the goal is to ride it off-road, but where can you do this legally. This is not as difficult as one might think, but you will have to put the mountain bike on a car and drive there. Therefore the first step is to acquire a rack for attaching the mountain bike to the car. There are a number of different types available:

- Roof rack bars on the roof and an attachment to stand bike on the bars
- Rack which attaches to the tow bar
- Rack which secures to any hatchback or rear of the car

If you go for the first option remember that you must be strong enough to lift the bike high into the air and onto the roof of the car. If you own a heavy mountain bike you might like to give this method a miss.

Many people carry their bike at the rear of their vehicle. If you choose this method then please ensure that you do it legally. The rear lights, especially the brake lights should not be obscured. Too many cars pass me with obscured registration plates or rear lights. Please get an inexpensive trailer board fitted if using a hatchback type mounting.

For tow bar owners a rack can be purchased that holds two or more bikes and attaches onto the tow bar. My mountain bike is transported using this method. If you own a four wheel drive where the spare wheel is mounted on the rear door. Finding a mount that projects over the spare wheel can be quiet a problem. Don't give up though, contact On the Ball bike racks who produce a number of different models.

Another very popular type of rack is that which holds two to four bikes and can be adjusted to rest at any angle on a hatchback or estate door. It always comes, with straps for attaching to the doors but my recommendation is to replace these with some ratchet straps instead.

Well the rack is on the car, can we go?

Before you set off stop to look at the clothing you are wearing. First of all get yourself a helmet. When you are riding through the woods it's easy to fall off suddenly (my favourite was riding too slow going around an obstacle!) or be hit by a branch, which is far more likely. So the moral of the story is, get a helmet, my preference is for the hard shell kind.

Anything else?

Yes, what have you got on your arms, legs and feet. Those slick cycle shorts look good but you won't catch me wearing them because they offer no protection against those friendly stinging nettles and thistles. Many of the routes in this guide involve cycling along paths which sometimes are slightly overgrown. So always protect the legs. In my experience it's not so important to keep the arms covered. However, after riding my bike for a few months, buying one of those bright yellow cycle jackets proved a wise investment. Why, so those day-dreaming car drivers might just see me.

An item that one should not be without is fingerless cycle gloves. They were the second accessory purchased after my helmet. Why, because they provide grip, are useful for pushing nettles out of the way and they help prevent the hands from being hurt by the bumps. On your feet a sturdy pair of shoes is a must. Trainers will suffice but when it's muddy in the woods, a good pair of walking boots are best.

Surely there is nothing else to take?

It's extremely easy to get lost when you start riding off-road routes. Despite the fact that most of these routes are on rights of way which should be marked. Frequently the signs are missing, or they are not marked at all, and when the route splits, which way does one go. The answer is to carry a good map from the Ordnance Survey. The best ones are the green Pathfinder series. My map is kept in one of those plastic map holders available from all good hiking shops which is thrown over my shoulder. You could also consider carrying a compass to get you out of trouble when the track comes to an end and you need to walk it! and believe me it does happen.

Can I go now please!

After riding for many months without trouble, two extra items were added to my bike. A pump to blow up the tyres and a cycle repair kit comprising of a range of tools such as allen keys, spanners, cycle rivet tool, patch repair kit and a few other items. So far I have had six punctures (all on the routes around Itchen Wood), on the first I had to walk home and of course was miles from the car, and once I fixed the tyre at the side of the road. A useful tip, when you do repair the puncture, don't forget to remove the cause, usually a thorn from the tyre. One last fun item, a cycle computer is worth considering. Facilities vary between models, but the basic items are speed, distance travelled, time on this ride, average speed and more sophisticated models include an altimeter (not necessary for these rides I can assure you). Don't forget to check the bike over. Is everything well oiled and greased, and tight?

Ok, it's time to go but take it easy the first few times. It can be tough riding sometimes, especially up hills. One final point, you might like to take some cleansing wipes with you. It is not uncommon to come out of the woods with a muddy bike, ride it down the road and get absolutely covered in mud, especially on your face! It only happened to me once, the following day a mud guard set appeared on my bike.

That's all folks, time to go riding and have fun!

Route Summary

Each route is numbered and the times shown for each route are for approximation purposes only because the time required will vary depending upon the individual rider and the conditions prevailing at the time the route is ridden. Nevertheless if you allow a maximum of one and a half hours then you should return to the start of the ride well before this period of time has expired.

Route Summary

Route No.	Description	Duration hrs:min	Dist miles	Map	Grade	Mud
1.	Itchen Wood	00:25	2.5	Pathfinder 1243	4	Yes
2.	Around Northington	00:45	7	Pathfinder 1243	4	No
3.	Itchen Stoke Down	00:55	6	Pathfinder 1243	3	No
4.	Abbotstone	00:55	7.25	Pathfinder 1243	3	No
5.	Closedown Wood	00:45	6	Pathfinder 1224	3	Yes
6.	Weston Common - Long Lane	01:00	6.5	Pathfinder 1224	2	Yes
7.	Weston Common	01:00	6.5	Pathfinder 1224	2	Yes
8.	Ox Drove	00:55	6.25	Pathfinder 1243	3	No
9.	Four Marks	00:55	5.75	Pathfinder 1244	3	Yes
10.	Yarmouth	00:50	6.75	Outdoor Leisure 29	3	No
11.	Ventnor	01:15	5.5	Outdoor Leisure 29	1	No
12.	Clearbury Ring	01:10	8	Pathfinder 1262	2	No
13.	Stratford Toney	01:15	6	Pathfinder 1262	2	Yes
14.	Whitsbury Down	00:50	6.25	Pathfinder 1262	4	No
15.	Knapp Down	01:00	7.5	Pathfinder 1262	3	No
16.	Ivy Wood	00:45	8.5	Outdoor Leisure 22	3	Yes
17.	Ashley heath	00:30	4.25	Outdoor Leisure 22	4	No
18.	Lepe	01:00	9.5	Outdoor Leisure 22	3	Yes
19.	Ringwood Forest	00:30	4	Outdoor Leisure 22	4	No
20.	Sutton Scotney	00:50	7.75	Pathfinder 1243	3	Yes

ROUTE SUMMARY

Route No.	Description	Duration hrs:min	Dist miles	Map	Grade	Mud
21.	Compton Down	00:50	6	Pathfinder 1264	3	No
22.	Longwood Warren	00:45	5.25	Pathfinder 1264	4	Yes
23.	Fawley Down	01:00	6.25	Pathfinder 1264	2	No
24.	Along the A33	01:10	6	Pathfinder 1188	3	Yes
25.	Stubbington Down	00:45	5.5	Pathfinder 1203	2	No
26.	Watership Down	01:15	6.75	Pathfinder 1203	1	No
27.	Queen Elizabeth Forest	00:45	7	Pathfinder 1285	1	Yes
28.	Stansted Forest	00:50	7	Pathfinder 1285	3	No

Grade: 1 - Difficult 2 - Hard 3 - Moderate 4 - Easy

Recommended Maps

Pathfinder

1188 Mortimer and Aborfield
1203 Kingclere & Ashmansworth
1224 Lasham & Alton
1243 Winchester (North)
1244 Alton & Four Marks
1262 Salisbury (South) & Broad Chalke
1264 Winchester (South)
1285 Horndean

Outdoor Leisure

22 New Forest
29 Isle of Wight

North Winchester. The track down from the wind pump

North Winchester

This is an excellent place to ride a mountain bike because there are many trails which intersect, offering the rider many variations on the rides described here.

Take the A33 road north from Winchester and at the first dual carriageway turn right at the Lunways Inn. Be careful turning right, it can only be achieved by moving into the right-hand lane and then moving into the turn right lane approximately half the length of the dual carriageway. A short distance along this road, after passing underneath the M3 motorway, on the left is Micheldever Wood which belongs to the Forestry Commission.

Stand with your back to the M3 motorway, the small Forestry Commission car park is located on the left-hand side of the road. Less than 100 metres from the car park on the right-hand side is the wide (usually muddy) entrance to the bridleway. This track is wide enough for vehicles and there are frequently a few parked here. This is the starting point for the rides in this chapter.

1: Itchen Wood

Duration: 25 minutes
Distance: 2.5 miles
Pathfinder Map: 1243
Start: GR533362
Type of Rode: Off road and mud likely
Grade: 4

This is a short route around fields and through Itchen Wood that is not very hard but enjoyable. Especially the downhill ride home. It is ideal for beginners provided it has not been raining recently. Although this route is

SOUTHERN COUNTIES BIKE GUIDE

very short, it's an ideal starters ride or twice around!

- Start at the **bridleway**.
- After negotiating the mud at the entrance, the track goes **between two fields** and then enters a **covered area** which is up a slight incline and then down. As you ride **down the slope** you will come into an **open area** and the **path divides**.
- Take the **turning to the right** which goes along the side of the field. Follow the path around the field and into the woods.
- Once **in the woods** it might be a bit muddy if it has been raining recently. The gate is probably locked, therefore you will have to dismount and pass through the **narrow entrance on the left.**

   When in the woods please keep on the path and be prepared to dismount and lift the bike over the trees that sometimes lie across the path. Remember that this route is a bridleway and you might meet a horse jumping over the tree!
- After a few minutes come out of the woods to an opening with paths on your left and right. Ignore these and **go straight**

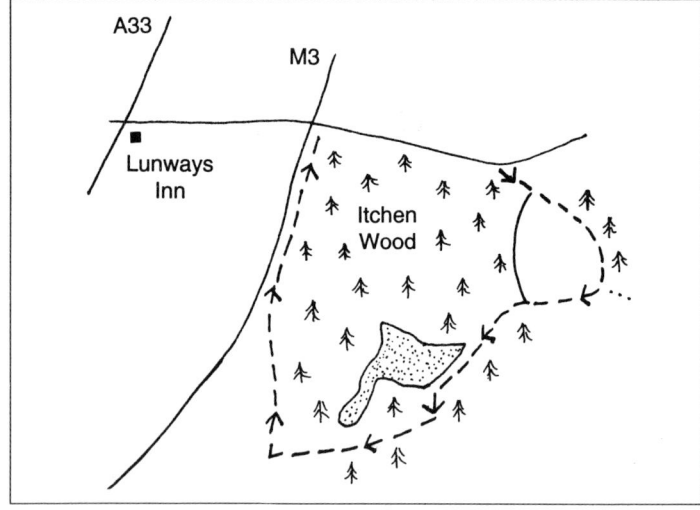

ahead. A word of warning here, this path is not used very often and it may look overgrown. If you look carefully there is an arrow for the bridleway on the right-hand side fence post.

- Follow this track which goes around the fields and eventually find yourself **back in the wood**. Once in the woods simply follow the track which bears around to the right and takes you through the wood to a **gate**. This track can be very muddy if it has been raining and, once again, expect to dismount and lift the bike over some tree trunks.

- At the gate, go through and **out onto the road** immediately ahead. There will be tracks on your left and right, ignore these and go **straight on**.

- At the end of the road, **turn right** and follow this road to the end. For some of the time you will be able to see the M3 motorway on your left.

- At the end of the road you will see to your left the bridge with the motorway above it, **turn right** and you will be back at your car.

2: Around Northington

Duration:	45 minutes
Distance:	7 miles
Pathfinder Map:	1243
Start:	GR533362
Type of Ride:	Mixture road and tracks
Grade:	4

This route is mainly road and gravel tracks which is ideal for beginners. Unfortunately it includes a few hills that will no doubt set the heart pounding, however it also includes some nice views at the top of most of the hills. At one of the main intersections you will probably hear a shooting party nearby.

- Start at the bridleway.
- After negotiating the mud at the entrance, the track goes **between two fields** and then enters a **covered area** which is up a slight incline and then down. As you ride **down the slope** you will come into an open area and the **path divides**.
- Take the **route to the left** which is a very wide track. After a few hundred yards this opens out into a narrow road. The road passes a hay barn on the right and at the **top of the hill** there is a wind pump on the left.
- Just past the hill the road bears to the right and there is a track on the left. Take the **left gravel track** and take care cycling down it.
- Follow the track which ends on a **minor road** called Northington Road
- **Cross the road** and just **ahead on the left is another track** which is a car's width and passes between two fields. This is the continuation of the bridleway.
- **Proceed straight** up here and as you come to the top of the hill,

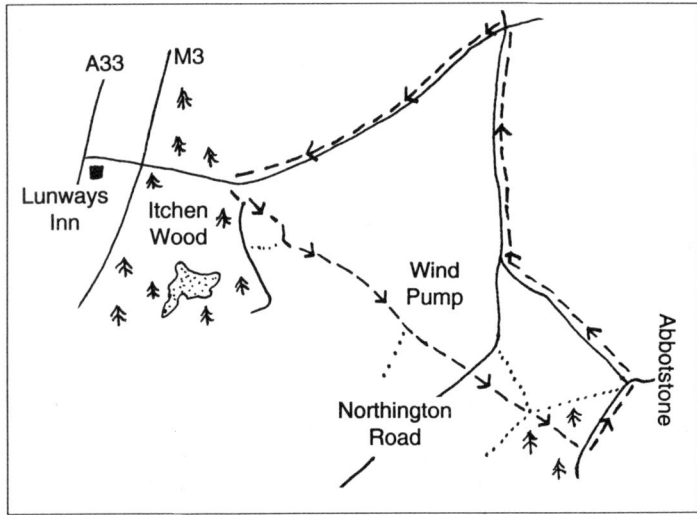

there will be an opening with 2 tracks on your left, one going back in a slightly different direction, one on the right and another straight ahead, but it is around the bend. This can be quite a confusing junction so take care here and watch out for horses.

- **Go straight ahead** (if you take the left track you will cut off part of the route).
- Cycle along this track and when you reach the road, **turn left**. Note there is a track in front of you but do not take it this time.
- Once on the road, cycle down the hill and at the junction **bear round to the left**. If you took the shortcut at the previous junction and took the left route you would come out here.
- Continue cycling along the road and when you reach the **end** and are exhausted after climbing the hill, **turn right** at the junction. This is Northington Road which we crossed earlier.
- Cycle along this road **until a junction** is reached where you must **turn left**. Don't be alarmed if you cycle some distance before getting to the end of this road. This country road has few distinguishing landmarks. At the junction turn left onto the main road and shortly you will be back where you started.

3: Itchen Stoke Down

Duration:	55 minutes
Distance:	6 miles
Pathfinder Map:	1243
Start:	GR533362
Type of Ride:	Mainly tracks, some roads
Grade:	3

This route is one of the author's personal favourites. It's a pleasant route comprising mainly of tracks and some road work. The steep hill climb up Rectory Lane makes up for all those food items one should not have consumed during the week. Be warned this is affectionately known as the "puncture" route. Thick spines frequent this route and they home in on mountain bike tyres.

- Start at the bridleway.
- After negotiating the mud at the entrance, the track goes **between two fields** and then enters a **covered area** which is up a slight incline and then down. As you ride **down the slope** you will come into an **open area** and the **path divides**
- Take the **route to the left** which is a very wide track. After a few hundred yards this opens out into a narrow road.
- The road passes a hay barn on the right and at the **top of the hill** there is a wind pump on the left.
- Just past the hill the road bears to the right and there is a track on the left. Take the **left track** and take care cycling down the gravel track.

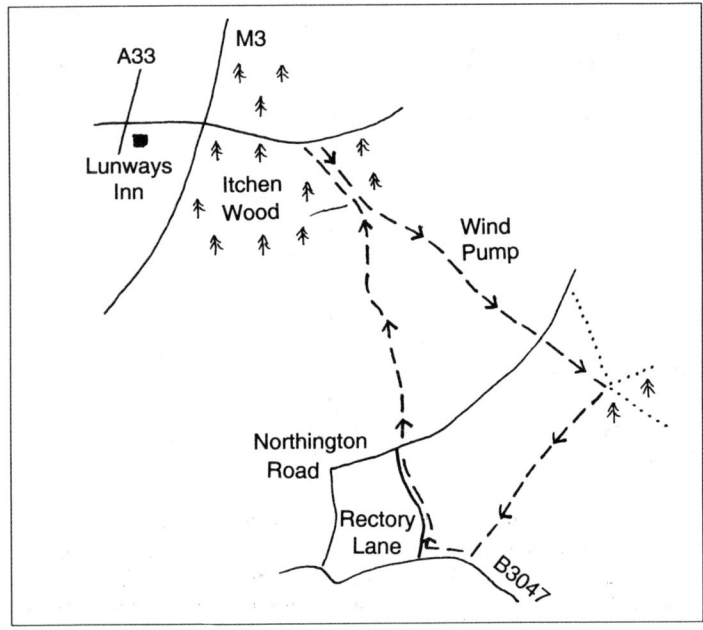

- Follow the track which **ends** on a **minor road** called Northington Road.
- **Cross the road** and just **ahead on the left is another track** which is a car width and passes between two fields. This is the continuation of the bridleway.
- **Proceed straight** up here and as you **come to the top of the hill**, there will be an opening with 2 tracks on your left, one going back in a slightly different direction, one on the right and another straight ahead, but it is around the bend. This can be quite a confusing junction so take care here and watch out for horses.
- Take the **track on the right**, and **ride it to the end**. The route passes between several fields, winds around, crosses a disused railway line and eventually winds down to the B3047.

    It's a real bone shaking ride and the thorns from the bushes are likely to puncture your tyres. Not wishing to put you off, the author has experienced at least 3 punctures riding this route, but it's worth it.
- The track emerges out onto the B3047. This is a very busy road so take care as you **turn right** onto the road.
- Cycle a short distance and **turn right into Rectory Lane**. It's time now to climb up the hill. This is a busy lane so watch out for cars.
- At the end of the lane there is track in front of you. **Go straight ahead** onto the bridleway, which is not signposted.
- Follow the bridleway, it does **bear to the right** after climbing yet another hill. Soon the track goes **downhill** and eventually comes out to a part of the route where we have been before (the wide track we cycled up to pass the wind pump).
- **Turn left** onto the wide track, cycle downhill.
- At the bend where there is a track to the left and one which bears to the right, **take the one to the right**.
- Now go up the hill you had so much fun riding down and then down the hill you hated riding up when we first started this ride. The end of this route returns us to the bridleway entrance where we first started.

SOUTHERN COUNTIES BIKE GUIDE

4: Abbotstone

Duration:	55 minutes
Distance:	7.25 miles
Pathfinder Map:	1243
Start:	GR533362
Type of Ride:	Downhill tracks and some road
Grade:	3

When cycling this route one can almost forget that large cities are close by. It's a delightful route, of mainly tracks which are predominantly downhill, although if exercise is required, do this route in reverse. The road work is limited so it can be considered a good off road route. During the summer listen out for the four wheel bike riders.

- Start at the bridleway.

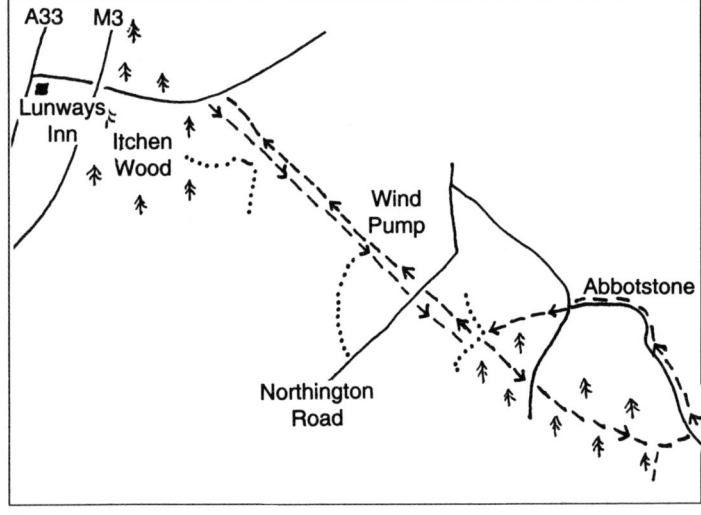

Junction near the watercress beds

- After negotiating the mud at the entrance, the track goes **between two fields** and then enters a **covered area** which is up a slight incline and then down. As you ride **down the slope** you will come into an **open area** and the **path divides**.
- Take the **route to the left** which is a very wide track. After a few hundred yards this opens out into a narrow road.
- The road passes a hay barn on the right and at the **top of the hill** there is a wind pump on the left.
- Just past the hill the road bears to the right and there is a track on the left. Take the **left track** and take care cycling down the gravel track. Follow the track which **ends** on a **minor road** called Northington Road.
- **Cross the road** and just **ahead on the left** is another track which is a car's width and passes between two fields. This is the continuation of the bridleway.
- **Proceed straight** up here and as you **come to the top** of the hill, there will be an opening with 2 tracks on your left, one going back in a slightly different direction, one on the right and

another straight ahead, but it is around the bend. This can be quite a confusing junction so take care here and watch out for horses.

- Take the track **straight ahead** which is around the bend. This is a wide track and watch out for walkers. The track comes out onto a minor road.

- At the road, there is another track, carefully cross the road and proceed **straight ahead**. This is a very long track but it is very enjoyable to ride. It is mainly downhill and is generally not very muddy. However, take care because sometimes people are living in caravans at the side of this track. At the bottom of the track, take a moment to view the watercress beds on the left.

- Cross over the river, come to a junction and take the **route to the left**. This is an uphill route, mainly of gravel, so watch don't slip.

- The track comes out onto the road, **turn left** and enjoy cycling on the country lane. It's hilly in places, so I suggest making good speed on the downhill legs. Follow the road down into Abbotstone, as you pass over the river the road bears to the right and left and there is a track immediately opposite.

- Take the **car width track opposite** which is a hilly climb to the top. Definitely one to get the heart pounding.

- At the top of the track, come to the junction that we met earlier. There are tracks on the left, straight ahead and around the bend on the right. **Bear right and then take the track straight ahead.**

- Now take the earlier route in reverse. Therefore **cycle this track to the road**, but enjoy cycling down the hill instead of up it.

- **Cross the road** and now its time to cycle up the gravel track immediately opposite. This track will definitely get the heart pounding.

- At the top of the track is the familiar wind pump. **Follow the track** past the wind pump, this time downhill, to the bend.

- At the bend **bear right** and follow this track to its end. Now back at the start of the ride.

Lasham

Lasham is probably best known as one of the main gliding centres in the United Kingdom. However for the mountain biker, if offers some splendid tracks and enjoys the dubious honour of the first place where one could lose one's way. The nice thing about cycling around here is that if all else fails, look in the sky and head in the direction of the gliders and aeroplanes. Not that you should ever have to resort to that tactic! The rides here will all take about an hour. They are predominantly off road and if you like mud, these are routes for you, but only if it has been raining!

One disadvantage of cycling in this area is that the routes are not very well marked and it is quite easy to think that one is lost. Recently Hampshire County Council carried out extensive work on the bridleways and they are easier to find. Nevertheless there is a distinct lack of signs and markers. If at any time you do feel lost, just follow the track to its end and civilisation should appear.

To reach Lasham, take the A339 from Basingstoke. This is a long road which passes through several villages. All the rides here originate close to Lasham Gliding Club. Therefore turn left on the first bend where there is a sign to Lasham and the Industrial Estate; this is Avenue Road. Continue along this road and past the sign for Lasham gliding, do not enter the airfield. Instead proceed past the gliding entrance and a little further along will find a small car park on the right-hand side which overlooks the airfield. All the routes will start from this point.

At weekends this car park is busy so please park thoughtfully. It is a very pleasant place to have lunch afterwards, and next door is an aircraft restoration society whose planes are well worth a visit.

SOUTHERN COUNTIES BIKE GUIDE

5: Closedown Wood

Duration: 45 minutes
Distance: 6 miles
Pathfinder Map: 1224
Start: GR692439
Type of Ride: Mud likely, roads, some hills
Grade: 3

Of the three routes in this area, this one is probably the easiest of them. If it has been raining then its likely to be quite muddy at the outset but eventually you will be back on gravel tracks and roads. It is also not too hilly and the Golden Pot pub is at the end of one hilly ride.

- Come out of this little car park and **turn right**.
- A short distance along this road, by the nurseries on the right, is an entrance into the wood **on the left**. It's a vehicle wide muddy track which may be signposted. Enter here and cycle to the end of the short track.
- Emerge onto one of the roads of the Forestry Commission. Turn **right** onto the track and almost immediately you will come to a fork.
- At the first fork take the **left route**
- At the next fork **bear right**.
  Now cycling along a rutted track, you will know that you are on the correct route because there should be lots of horses tracks here. This track is fun and if it has been raining it will be very muddy. After approximately 8 minutes, the track will end and there will be a gate.
- **At the gate** which denotes the end of the Forestry Commission land there are two bridleway tracks on the left. Ignore these, **go through the gate** and don't forget to close it behind you.
- Now you will be **cycling on a road** and just past the gate is a

private residence on the left.
- Continue along the road, at the **first junction go straight on**, the tracks on the left and right are private roads.
- The road will shortly **change into a track**. Then **reach another junction**.
- Here there are a number of routes to chose from. Look to your **right** for a road and also, **heading at almost right angles** to the track you have just come along, another grassed track. **Take the grassed track**, not the road.
- Now cycle down this grassed track until you reach the **main road**, the B3349
- **Turn right** onto the B3349 road and cycle uphill.

  This is one of those routes that passes a local watering hole, and since almost at the end of your ride, provides an ideal excuse, if one is needed, to stop for a well deserved drink. But remember even cyclists should not drink and drive!
- At the **Golden Pot** pub **turn right**, there is also a sign here to Lasham Gliding.

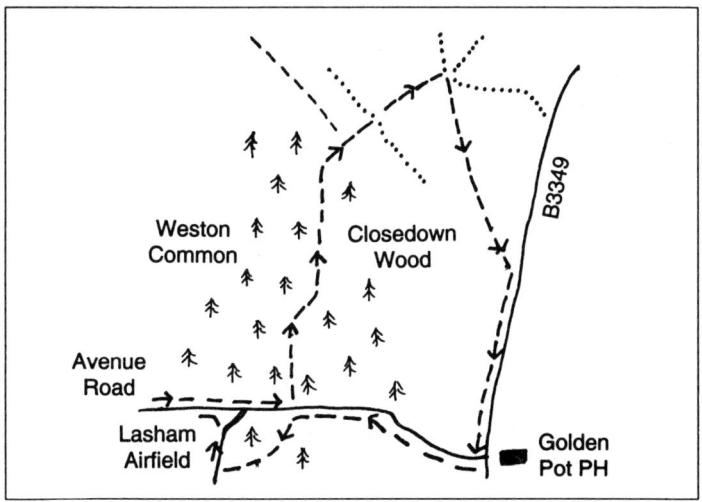

SOUTHERN COUNTIES BIKE GUIDE

- Cycle along this road, just **past the nursery** to reach the point at which you entered the woods initially, which is now on your right. Almost immediately opposite on the **left-hand side** is an entrance to a field and another bridleway just to the right.
- **Turn left** onto the bridleway by the gate and cycle along this potentially muddy path.
- Some way through the wood you will come to a **sort of junction** where there is a footpath path sign on your left. **Proceed straight ahead here** and continue until you get to the road.
- At the **road turn right** and cycle to the end **where you turn left** and return to where you first started from (which will be on the left).

6: Weston Common - Long Lane Track

Duration:	1hr
Distance:	6.5 miles
Pathfinder Map:	1224
Start:	GR692439
Type of Ride:	Mud likely and gravel tracks
Grade:	2

This is a fun route but if it has been raining you might wonder why you bothered at the outset. The first five minutes can be very muddy, but after that it's downhill all the way on a lovely track. Then just a short distance along the road before venturing onto another track there is a hilly climb through the woods before returning to the Forestry Commission land and more mud.

- Come out of this little car park and **turn right**.
- A short distance along this road, just before the nurseries on

LASHAM

the right is an official entrance on the left with a sign to the Oil Company. **Take this entrance** and just before their private road is the bridleway on the left.

- **Turn left** onto this track. It's very rutted with deep tractor tracks and presents a very interesting challenge to the mountain bike rider, especially if has been raining recently because it will be very, very muddy. Don't be surprised if you have to dismount and walk some of this track. When it has been raining the tracks can be very deep.

- This is a very long track, don't be tempted to deviate onto any of the other routes. Simply follow this track to the end which eventually comes out onto **Bagmore Lane**.

- **Turn right** onto the road and cycle a short distance to the junction with a **sign to Weston**.

- **Turn right** into Weston village and proceed up the incline past some houses.

- At the point where the road bears to the left, **on the bend is a**

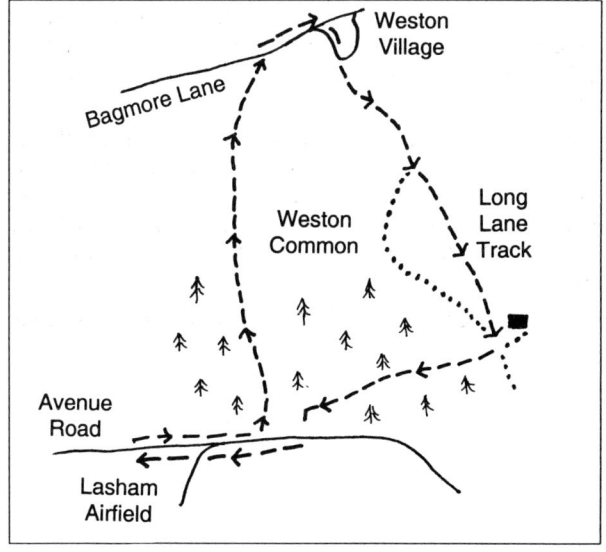

track with a large sign advising no vehicular access. Take the track ahead and start cycling uphill again, sorry!

- At the **top of the hill** the track finishes and joins a road which has originated from the left. **Proceed onto the road** and at the first bend stop.
- The road bears to the right, but on the **left** is a track which rises up towards a wood. **Take this track, known as Long Lane**, but don't look for a sign!
- To verify you are on the right track, you should cycle **underneath the electricity pylon** before you pass the wood on the left.
- Keep following the track and eventually comes out with tracks on your left, right and straight ahead. The ones on the left and right are private and the **narrow track ahead** is the one you require.
- **Cycle straight ahead** and follow the track until it comes out by the house in the Closedown Wood route.
- **Turn right** onto the Forestry Commission track. Now you will probably meet some humans. The track is wide, likely to be muddy and has routes coming off of it. Please stick to the bridleway, you don't need any of these other routes to have fun.
- It's a long track and eventually comes out on another route. **Bear right** and you will quickly see a **track directly on your left**. Cycle this short route and come out onto the main road. Don't be tempted to ignore this last route and cycle to the end of the road. The gate at the end of the Forestry Commission track is locked.
- **Turn right** onto the road and back to where you started.

7: Weston Common

Duration: 1hr
Distance: 6.5 miles
Pathfinder Map: 1224
Start: GR692439
Type of Ride: Mud likely and gravel tracks
Grade: 2

This route is very similar to the Long Lane track but it has been included because it is an interesting variation on the previous route. The same warnings about mud and hills still apply. One should also be warned that this is probably one of the few routes where one could get lost because there is one part that is not very well marked. Suggest taking an OS map along on this ride.

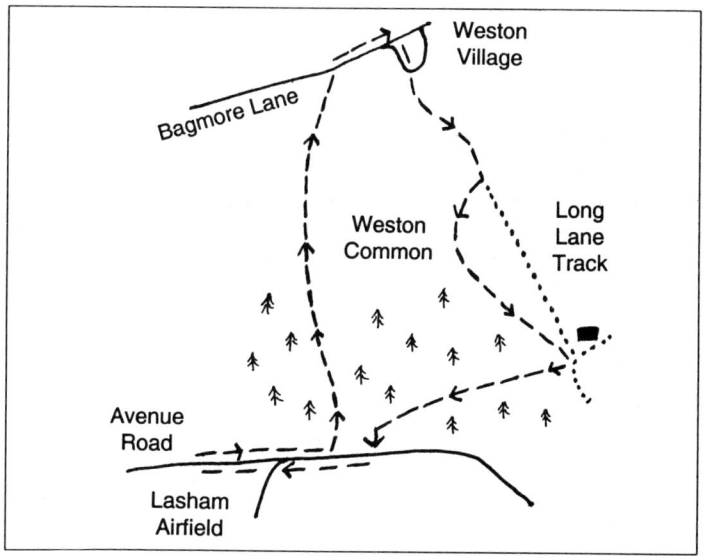

- Come out of this little car park and **turn right**.
- A short distance along this road, just before the nurseries on the right, is the road to the Oil Company. **Take this entrance** and just before their private road is the bridleway on the left.
- **Turn left** onto this track. It's very rutted with deep tractor tracks and presents a very interesting challenge to the mountain bike rider. Especially if has been raining recently because it will be very, very muddy.
- This is a very long track, don't be tempted to deviate onto any of the other routes. Simply follow this track to the end which eventually comes out onto **Bagmore Lane**.
- **Turn right** onto the road and cycle a short distance to the junction with a **sign to Weston**.
- **Turn right** into Weston village and proceed up the incline past some houses.
- At the point where the road bears to the left, **on the bend is a track with a large sign advising no vehicular access**. Take the track ahead and start cycling uphill again, sorry!
- At the **top of the hill** the track finishes and joins a road which has originated from the left. **Proceed onto the road and at the first bend stop**.
- Follow the road around as it **bears to the right**, ignoring the track on the left which is Long Lane.
- After some distance the road ends. Immediately ahead is an opening to a farmers field, a track on the right and a **track almost ahead on the left, but straight ahead**. Take the one straight ahead. This route is an uphill climb which narrows as it enters the woods. On summer days this offers some shade from the sun and is never muddy in winter.

    At the entrance to the woods, take care, the track is not well marked.
- **Turn left** and hopefully you should see a wide path, but don't worry if its not too well marked. Proceed for about 100yds, then **turn right**, where will see a large tree trunk blocking the way.

The downhill run from the windpump near Winchester (Routes 2,3,4)
The narrow Rookwood Lane track (Route 9)

The cottages by the Ford at Stratford Toney (Route 13)
The coastal path towards Ventnor (Route 10)

- Horse riders jump over the tree trunk, but I suggest you **dismount and walk around it**.
- The track becomes **very wide**, it is also likely to be very muddy. Cycle down this route, then up and you will come out by a house and a gate on your left.
- **Turn right** onto the Forestry Commission tracks. Now you will probably meet some humans. The track is wide, likely to be muddy and has routes coming off it. Please stick to the bridleway, you don't need any of these other routes to have fun.
- It's a long track and eventually come out on another route. **Bear right** and you will quickly see a **track directly on your left**. Cycle this short route and will come out onto the main road. Don't be tempted to ignore this last route and cycle to the end of the road. The gate at the end of the Forestry Commission track is locked.
- **Turn right onto the road** and now back to where you started.

Alresford

Alresford is probably best described as a traditional English village on the A31 a short distance east of Winchester. After the rides described here, stop in the village and take a stroll around, there are some delightful shops and places to eat.

8: Ox Drove

Duration:	55 minutes
Distance:	6.25 miles
Pathfinder Map:	1243
Start:	GR585361
Type of Ride:	Mainly wide tracks
Grade:	3

This route is not very hard and offers some nice views of the local villages. It's part of the Ox Drove track so it's fun looking out for the signs along this route. Most of the route is along gravel tracks, but there is a short piece of road work and some gentle hills to climb.

Take the B3046 north out of Alresford, first passing through the old small village of Old Alresford, then opening into countryside. Shortly come to Abbotstone Down where there are car parks on both the left- and right-hand side of the road. Park on either side but the route starts on the right.

- On the **right-hand side** there is a sign for the Ox Drove track. You will see this small animal sign on all subsequent Ox Drove signs.

- Follow the signs for the Ox Drove track. This is a very popular area so it is very likely will meet walkers, dogs (not on leads) and horse riders. Stay on the track which **bears around to the left** and through a field and comes out on a gravel road. Stop here for a moment and admire the view.

- Proceed **straight ahead** onto the gravel path. It now bears around to the left and comes out onto another road. At this point the road on the left is marked as private, so **proceed ahead** and to the left.

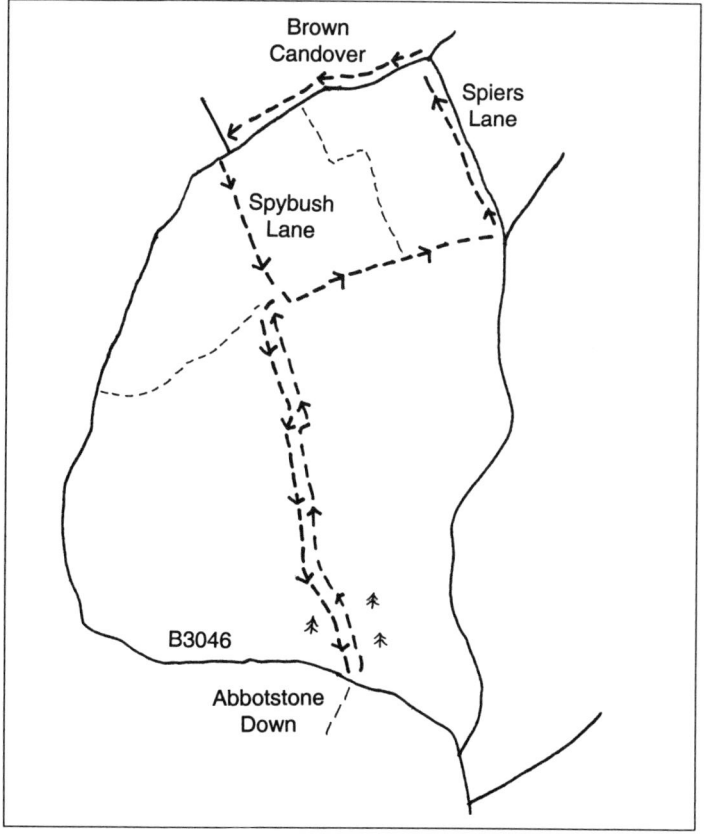

Spybush Lane part of the Wayfarer's Walk

This track is uphill, but it doesn't take its toll too much. Follow the track around to the left and at the top of the hill stop and look at Northington church in the distance.

- Follow the track downhill and stop at the bottom by the farm buildings. The route on the left is the Wayfarer's Walk, **turn right** and up to the next junction where there is a sign pointing in three directions.

    Look at the sign and you will see the animal logo for the Ox Drove track again.

- **Turn right** to follow the Ox Drove track which is slightly uphill. At one point you will see a route emerging on the left and a sign pointing straight on for the Ox Drove track. Carry straight on.

- This track comes out onto a road. **Turn left** onto the road and enjoy cycling downhill. It's a narrow lane so there's only enough room for a car and bicycle. At the end of the road at the Give Way sign, **turn left**.

    Cycle into the village of Brown Candover. Stop to admire the church and beautifully kept village green.

- There is a turning on the right called Gunners Lane, just past on the left is a very wide opening, this is Spybush Lane, **turn left** here. You will know if you have the correct spot because there is a phone box here. Cycle up the lane and return to the farm buildings we met earlier.

    Now back at the junction with the three-way sign.
- **Turn right** at the junction, cycle past the farm buildings and then **turn left** at the next junction.
- Now on the route we took earlier follow it **back to the start of the route**. That's up the hill, follow the track around which bears right then left. Down the hill and then, as the track bears right, go straight ahead because the right route is marked as private.
- **Straight ahead** and up the incline, the track bears to the left, then comes out into the open. Follow it into the wood and bear to the right to return to the car park.

9: Four Marks

Duration:	55 minutes
Distance:	5.75 miles
Pathfinder Map:	1244
Start:	GR691356
Type of Ride:	Hilly and mud likely
Grade:	3

This route will hopefully justify the purchase of your mountain bike. Although it does involve some road work, the routes are predominantly downhill along narrow tracks with overhanging branches. Unfortunately the rights of way are not well marked. At some points you may encounter some mud and have to dismount or get stuck. Don't miss the opportunity to wave to the passengers on the Mid-Hants railway as you cycle underneath the line.

Take the A31 from Winchester in the direction on Alton. Take the bypass around Alresford and pass through Ropley village. At the end of Ropley village the road changes into a dual carriageway. As the road bends to the left there is a turning on the left, turn left onto Grosvenor Road. Pass under a railway bridge which belongs to the Mid-Hants railway and hopefully you will see the old trains on the restored line. Continue past the houses and come to a junction, turn sharp left onto Stancombe Lane. Follow the lane as it bears around to the right, don't take the road straight ahead (it's a dead end). The road is straight then bears left and comes to a four-way junction. Turn left onto Lower Paice Lane. As the lane comes to an end and turns right into West End Lane, the route starts on the left.

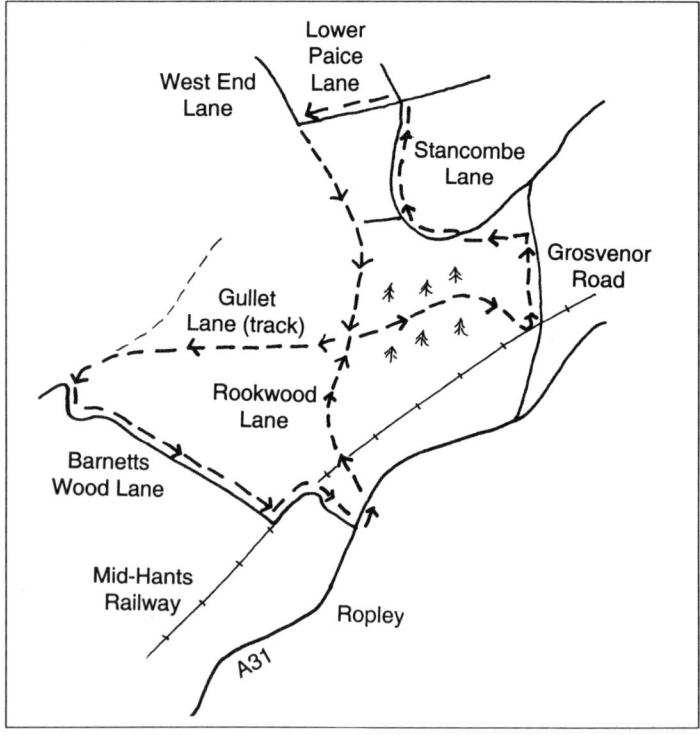

ALRESFORD

Gullet Lane track

- **On the left** is the opening to a farmer's field and the track is next to the field, please don't go into the field. The track, known as Rookwood Lane, is narrow and covered and fun. Follow the narrow track which goes up and down hill to its end where it comes out onto a road.
- **Cross the road** and proceed onto the track opposite.
  This track initially bears right and passes some houses. Then it narrows and is a fun downhill route.
- Eventually the track opens out at a four-way junction. Remember this location because we will return here later. Turn onto the **right track** which is Gullet Lane.
- Follow Gullet Lane which is a long track, mainly downhill. Just before the end the track bears to the left and there is a small route straight ahead. **Take the route straight ahead.** This track goes a short distance and then bears sharp right. The bend is likely to be very muddy, so look for alternative route which should be easily visible.

- As you come around the bend, the route ends with turnings on the left and right, **take the left route** and follow it down to the road.
- At the road, **turn left** and follow this road until it comes out onto the A31 main road. This is a long road so don't think you have taken the wrong way.

  You will pass Ransconbe Farm on the left and, if they are running, should hear and maybe see the trains on the Mid-Hants railway line. Shortly before reaching the A31 you will pass underneath a railway bridge.
- When you reach the A31, **turn left** and cycle about 50yds. Just before the bend there is an opening on the left where there is a field and a right of way entrance.

  The right of way sign is hidden in the hedgerow, but the path is clearly visible to the left of the farmer's field.
- **Turn left** onto the track and cycle up the hill and underneath the railway bridge. Here is a good place to stop and watch the trains go by.

Trains from the Mid-Hants Railway passing overhead

- Now follow this track until you reach the four-way junction where we turned left earlier. At the junction **turn right** onto the other part of the Gullet Lane track. Follow this track which is uphill and appears to be rather long. At one point the track opens with routes on the left and right. On the left is a footpath which crosses a field.
- At the junction **proceed straight on**. At this point the track may be very rutted and muddy.
  Follow this route to the very end where it comes out at the railway bridge on Grosvenor Road.
- **Turn left** onto Grosvenor Road and cycle up the road, past some houses and then you will see a bridleway sign on the left.
- **Turn left** onto the bridleway which goes uphill. Follow it to the end and you will see the stile for the other end of the footpath we met earlier. **Turn right** at the bend and proceed to Grosvenor Road, met earlier.
- **Turn left** onto Grosvenor Road and proceed to the junction with Lower Paice Lane. **Turn left** and return to the start of the ride.

The Isle of Wight

The Isle of Wight offers some great places to go cycling. There are some nice easy routes for the beginner or those out for a leisurely ride. If one heads south down towards St Catherine's Point, there are some hills and tracks to challenge the most enthusiastic mountain bike rider.

Travel to the island could not be easier. There are numerous ferries and the vehicle ones allow you to take the bike. You can take the easy option and attach the bike to the car, or leave the car at the port and cycle onto the ferry. The latter option is much cheaper, but it does restrict where you can go in the island. Look out for special one day offers for a car and several passengers.

Travelling around the island is easy, but remember there are no motorways. An excellent reference document is the Ordnance Survey Outdoor Leisure map 29 for the Isle of Wight. It details all the car parks and shows many routes for both walkers and cyclists.

Approaching the Isle of Wight on the ferry from Southampton

ISLE OF WIGHT

10: Yarmouth

Duration: 50 min
Distance: 6.75 miles
Map: Outdoor Leisure 29
Start: GR355896
Type of Ride: Track and road
Grade: 3

This is a pleasant ride which initially is flat and along an old disused railway line. On a nice summer's day it is very pleasant indeed. Next comes the hard climb up a hill, then its downhill to return along the disused railway track. This is a circular route to avoid excessive road work.

Drive towards the Yarmouth ferry and park in the car park on the bend, don't forget to pay the small parking fee.

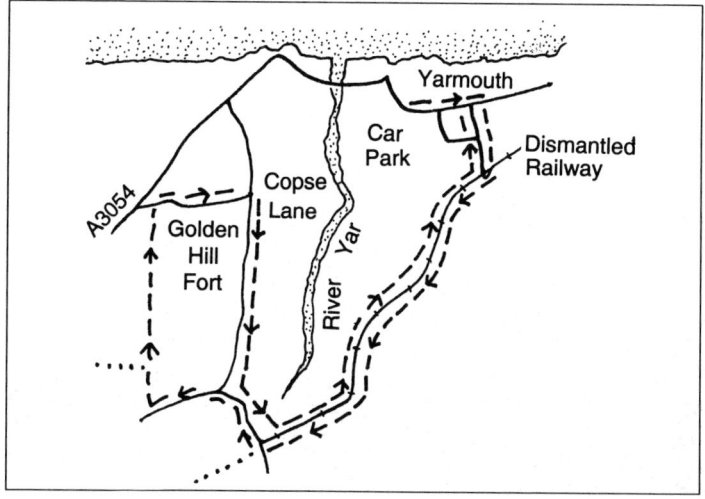

- Proceed out of the car park **onto the main road and take the 2nd turning on the right which is Victoria Road** and ride to the end of this road, where the road connects with the bridleway.

  Be careful, the bridleway may be hidden by the parked cars and trees!

- **Turn right** onto the Bridleway F61 (which is an old disused railway track) and cycle its length. This is a flat and easy ride. It's very pleasant but watch out for the walkers. The track runs along the river.

  Approximately 15 minutes later the track comes to its end where there is a road, a little bridge on the left and a track on the opposite side of the road. Don't continue on the bridleway.

- **Turn right** onto the road and cycle to the end of it.

  Remember this junction because you will return here later on the ride.

- **Turn left** onto the road, then take the **first turning on the right**, which is **Orchard Close**. Cycle to the end of this road which is marked as No Through Road where you should see a bridleway sign.

Yarmouth, dismantled railway

Looking down on Ventnor from Stenbury Down

- **Turn left again onto Bridleway F17** which is marked as School Green Road and Golden Hill. Cycle on the **bridleway** for several minutes, until you come to a **junction of paths**. If you miss the turning you will come to a No Cycling sign.
- The bridleway you require is the **track on the right**. The signpost is slightly misleading because it is located after the track.
- **Turn right** onto the bridleway and cycle up the hill. The track passes Golden Hill fort but you won't see it. This is hilly but a good climb.

  Some distance along this route there is a turning on the right marked as a circular route which goes around the fort and offers some nice views of the surrounding area.
- At the end of the bridleway **turn left** which takes you out onto the road and up to the main road.
- At the main road there is a turning on the right signposted to Norton Green. **Turn right** here and cycle to the end which joins with Copse Lane.

- **Turn right** onto Copse Lane and follow this route to the bend where there is a signpost for Freshwater and Totland. Remember this is the junction met before.
- At the bend **turn left** into Church Place. Cycle along this road until you return to the bridleway cycled earlier.
- **Turn left** onto the bridleway and cycle for about 15 minutes until you reach the point entered. If you need a landmark it is where the houses are by the bridleway and there is a sign there.
- **Turn left** back onto Victoria Road and cycle to the end. **Turn left** again onto the main road and then cycle a short distance to the car park.

11: Ventnor

Duration: 1hr 15 mins
Distance: 5.5 miles
Map: Outdoor Leisure 29
Start: GR548769
Type of Ride: Hilly
Grade: 1

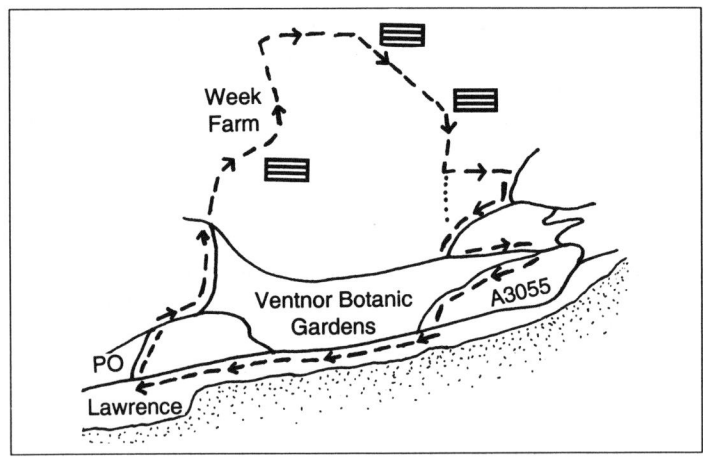

The view from the top of the hill is splendid, unfortunately the climb to get there is not. This is probably the most hilly route in the guide, so be sure to take plenty of water with you. The author had to dismount and walk often on this route but remembers it for the incredible speed achieved on the road back to the start.

This is a trail for those who want a hilly challenge or like to do a bit of walking. Park in the Botanic Gardens and don't forget to pay the parking fee. When you return this is a nice place to have a picnic in the designated area and investigate the gardens.

- Cycle out of the car park and **turn left** onto the road.
- Proceed along the road to St Lawrence. At the St Lawrence Inn pub **turn right** onto Spindlers Road. There should also be a sign here to the post office.
- Cycle up the hill and **turn right** at the top of the road onto Seven Sisters Road.
  Stop to admire some of the cottages in this area.
- Proceed along this road until you see a **turning on the left** with a limited width access sign, take this very hilly road. It is very steep, so be prepared to walk, unless you are fit of course! Once at the top of the hill, it's a great ride down.
- Stop at the junction and cycle across to **Weal Lane**. At the farm entrance cycle on and you will come to a junction where some bridleways are marked.
- **Bear to the right** and pass the farm buildings. Please close the gate after you.
- Now this is a real dirt track rutted hilly climb. Initially it starts as a gravel track, then it changes to a grassy track. At the **top of the hill**, you will come to a bridleway sign and will see another bridleway from the left. **Turn right** onto Bridleway V58 which is signposted Wroxall. This is another hilly climb which is no more than a track across a field.
- At the gate, go through and **turn right** onto Bridleway V63, signposted Upper Ventnor. At the top of the hill, admire the view, in the distance you can see the radio masts. Enjoy cycling along this narrow track and go **straight through** the gate.

- Pass **through the gate**, closing it behind you, and cycle on further down.

    The bridleway is adjacent to a golf course. Watch out for flying golf balls. If you are lucky you might find one, the author did. It's downhill all the way but stop to admire the spectacular view a few times. Look at the sign by the stile which says "Beware of Flying Golf Balls".

- Eventually coming to a **fork, take the left-hand** bridleway onto V54, signposted Upper Ventnor. This route travels along the edge of the hill. Once again stop to admire the view.

- This track will come out onto an access road. **Turn right** onto bridleway V54, signposted Steephill Down Road.

- At the end of the road **turn right** and travel a short distance and at the bend *turn right* again onto Gills Cliff Road. This is a long road, watch out for another sign to the Botanic Gardens on the right.

- Follow the road to the end, then **turn right** and cycle back to the Botanic Gardens.

    It's downhill all the way and you can really get speed up, so be careful!

The route across the fields after Wick Down (Route 12)
Ford and bridge across the Lymington River (Route 16)

The Isle of Wight from Lepe beach (Route 18)
Stubbington Down (Route 25)

Salisbury

As any true mountain biker will tell you, finding good routes can prove difficult. While in a book shop one day looking at the Ordnance Survey Pathfinder maps, I came across Salisbury (South) and Broad Chalke, Pathfinder 1262. Opening it there was an abundance of green routes, instantly it was obvious that this would be a great place to ride. This area is very similar to the routes around North Winchester, the routes shown here are but a few of the many possible variations.

This is a popular area, so expect to meet walkers and horse riders. It offers a mixture of both off road riding, climbing and descending hills and some road riding. Although the routes are mainly gravel tracks, some parts can be very muddy. Most of these routes are an ideal place for beginners, but some of them are poorly marked.

One final point, whilst writing this book I discovered that some of the routes had changed their usage as shown on the OS map.

Clearbury Ring as it appears at the start of the route

12: Clearbury Ring

Duration:	1hr 10 mins
Distance:	8 miles
Pathfinder Map:	1262
Start:	GR136235
Type of Ride:	Mainly roads, gravel tracks, hilly
Grade:	2

This route offers some interesting views of the surrounding area. Encountering mud is unlikely but a number of hills have to be climbed. Definitely a route to provide exercise.

Drive into Odstock village from Nunton using the turning on the A338. At the junction in the village turn left and pass the pub. Climb up the hill and follow the road until you come to a junction. There is a road on the left which returns you to Odstock village. The road on the right is private and straight ahead there is a wide dirt track road. Proceed onto the dirt track road ahead and just before the road bears to the right, there is a wide opening and a track on the left. On the entrance post there is a blue bridleway sign, the ride starts here!

- **Follow the track** and when you come to a gate go through it, but keep to the **track on the left**. There is one to the right but ignore it.
- The **left track climbs up the hill**. It is steep and probably needs first gear and several stops! At the top, or probably before, stop and admire the view. Use it as an excuse to have a drink.
- The track **bears to the right** and encircles the wood known as Clearbury Ring. Half way around there is a gate. **Go through the gate** and continue around the wood.
    If it has been raining recently this part is likely to be muddy!
- After circling the wood, the **track turns right and heads downhill**.

- Soon it comes to an **opening** where the track goes to the right. **Stop here and turn left**.

    Behind you there is a post indicating where the bridleway is but it can be rather confusing at this point.

- Approach the gate but do not go through, the bridleway follows the **edge of the field**. Now it's downhill all the way!

- Although a **downhill route**, the track does **turn left and then downhill again**. At the bottom, don't turn right, in the corner is the official bridleway entrance and gate.

- Go through the gate and you are now on the **A338** main road. **Turn right** onto the main road and cycle to **Downton** village which takes about eight minutes.

    Take care cycling along this very busy main road. Of course if already tired you could make a quick refreshment stop at the

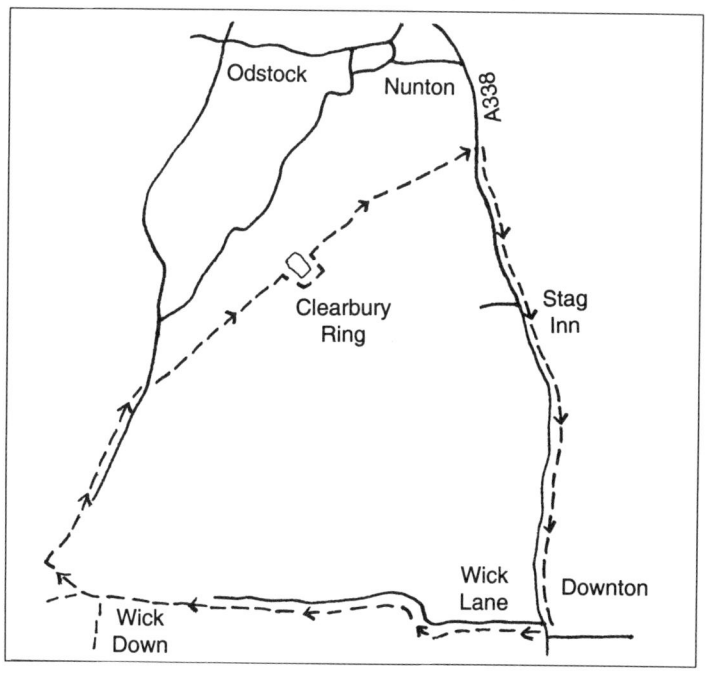

Stag Inn on the left on the road to Downton village.

- Go through the village, pass the petrol station, then **turn right** immediately into Wick Lane.
- Wick Lane starts off as a road and does at one point turn sharp right. Keep **following the road** and climbing up the hill! Eventually the road finishes and changes into a big wide road track, continue **straight ahead**.
- Then come to an opening on the **right**, the track passes between two fields. On the post there is a faint blue bridleway marker. Follow the track **across the field**, it's vehicle wide, and it comes out onto the gravel road.

  To verify you have taken the correct right turning, you should see a large barn to your right in the distance.

- Once at the gravel road, **turn right** and follow the road back to the point where the route started.

13: Stratford Toney

Duration:	1hr 15 mins
Distance:	6 miles
Pathfinder Map:	1262
Start:	GR101237
Type of Ride:	Tracks, roads, mud likely
Grade:	2

In contrast to the Clearbury Ring route, this route is mainly over tracks and could be very muddy in places. It's memorable for the river which has to be crossed and the very long byway afterwards that seems to go for ever and it's uphill. There are some scenic views at the beginning and during the short ride in the village of Coombe Bissett. It may be Route 13 but it should not be considered unlucky.

SALISBURY

From Salisbury take the A354 to arrive in the delightful village of Coombe Bissett, pass through and out of the village. As you climb up the hill, the road bears to the right and there is a road straight ahead where there is a sign to the Roman Villa. Go straight ahead, at the top of the hill, you will see signs on your left to the Caravan Park and Greenacres Park and a very wide gravel track on the left. The route starts here. Please don't park here and cause an obstruction, this track is well used by the residents whose houses are on this road and by motorists pulling caravans to the caravan park.

- **Opposite the gravel track** is a track a car's width. According to the OS map it's a byway, but it's not marked and at the other end of the track is shown as a bridleway. Cycle along this route.

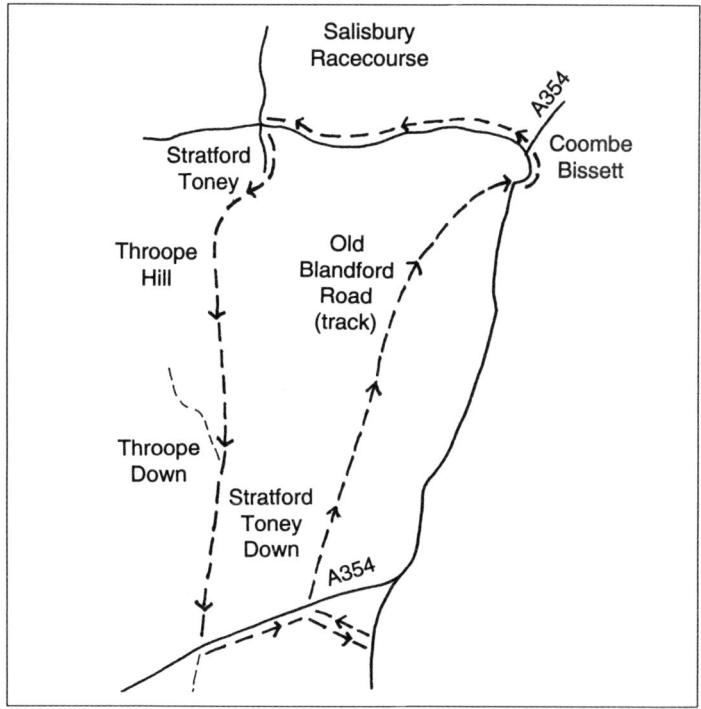

The River Ebbie passing through Coombe Bissett

SALISBURY

If it's been raining it will be a bit muddy. After a few minutes come out onto the A354 road.

- **Cross the A354 road** and enter the track on the opposite side of the road. There is a blue bridleway marker on the post. This is the Old Blandford Road track.
- As you enter the track, only go a short distance and the route turns **sharply left** into the field. This route now follows the edge of the field so keep left. The track passes through several fields, but if you keep left and follow the vehicle tracks you will be safe. Pass through several open gates and eventually come to a gate where there is a gravel road on the left.
- **Turn left onto the gravel road**. Now its downhill all the way. Please be careful as you cycle past the Cranbourne Farms building. The tracks comes out onto the A354 road by the church in Coombe Bissett.
- **Turn left** onto the A354, cycle around the bend, admiring the River Ebbie on your left. As you come out of the bend, take the first **turning on the left,** signposted to Stratford Tony. This road is called Stratford Tony Road.
- Cycle along this road for a little less than a mile. You will **come to a junction** with signs on the left pointing to Stratford Tony, and one on the right to Wilton. **Turn left** into Stratford Tony, there is a post box on the corner.
- This no through road leads to the tiny village of Stratford Tony. As you enter the village the byway sign points straight ahead; follow this sign to the River Ebbie. There is a footbridge, but it is *private so please do not use it*. Of course you could cycle through the river. If you are like me and don't want to get wet take the alternative route.

   The dry route is to turn right and cycle on the road, which leads to a small bridge which crosses the river. Then follow the track round to the left, pass the houses and back onto the byway.
- The byway would be the route to follow had you decided to go through the river.
- Once on this track which goes uphill, it comes to a junction

The River Ebbie and Coombe Bridge in Coombe Bissett

where another route bears to the left. Take the **left route** which is the byway.

- This is a very long byway, it will take about 35 minutes to cycle to its end. It starts as a hilly climb and seems to go on forever. At the top of the hill it flattens out and there is a brief opportunity to admire the hills. There are not too many opportunities to take alternate routes on this byway, but always keep going straight ahead. Eventually come out onto the A354 by the Coombe Hill Garage.

- **Turn left** onto the main road. As you cycle underneath the electricity pylon, you will come to the bridleway entrance met at the beginning of the ride where we crossed this road.

- **Turn right** onto the bridleway and cycle to the end, back at the point where the route started.

SALISBURY

14: Whitsbury Down

Duration: 50 minutes
Distance: 6.25 miles
Pathfinder Map: 1262
Start: GR136235
Type of Ride: Mainly gravel tracks
Grade: 4

This is an excellent route for beginners or someone wanting an easy ride. The route is mainly on very easy gravel tracks although there is one junction which could be muddy. The views of the tracks used by the racehorses are well worth a stop and there are few hills to climb.

Start this route at the same point as that for Clearbury Ring.

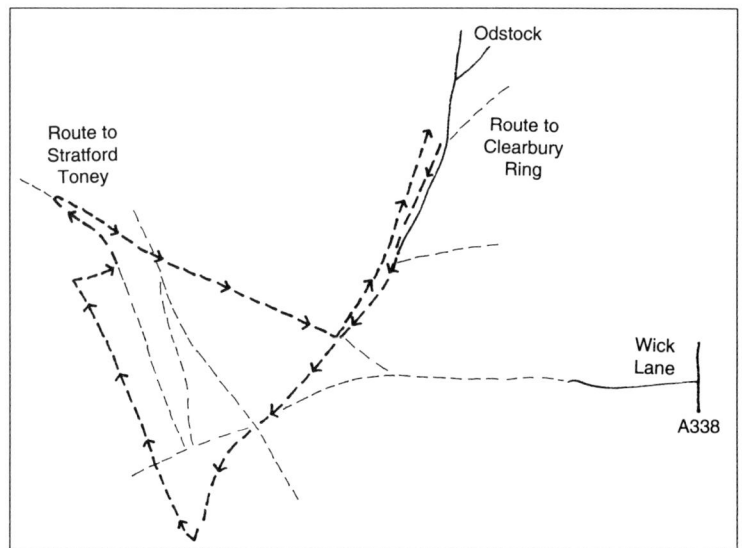

Whitsbury Down, the final track across the field

- Don't take the track for Clearbury Ring, instead follow the **gravel track**. This is the first of many gravel tracks, with a slight downhill incline. You will pass a barn on the left and eventually come out to a junction of byways and bridleways.

    At the junction a bridleway merges from the left. This area is likely to be very rutted and muddy, proceed with care and don't be afraid to get off and push if it's too deep and muddy. If it is difficult it's only a short distance.

- Once through the junction you will see routes on your left and right and one straight ahead. **Proceed straight ahead**, stopping for a moment to check that no racehorses are crossing the route.

- Now **cycle up the hill**, along the way other tracks will meet this route and at one point it will open out into a wide area. Continue straight ahead, passing the farm buildings on the left.

- At the road **turn right**, enjoy cycling the tarmac. The route is downhill and one can get some speed up here, but watch out for walkers and dogs not on leads. Now follow this track to its end. Along the way you will pass several other tracks and on your left is Whitsbury Down. At one point the **track bears sharp right**, just follow it. It will also change from a road to a gravel track.

Adjacent to the road is a track for racehorses, so look out for a future winner passing you by.

- Eventually the track comes to an end, where there are routes to your left and right. There is also a sign for each of the byways. **Turn left here**.

- Proceed along this track. At one point it might be rutted and muddy for a short distance. Then it will **bear sharp right** just before the end where it will join with another route. **Turn right here** (if you went left, you would come out at the starting point for the Stratford Toney route).

- This is a lovely car width track to cycle since it's not too inclined or rutted. In a few minutes the track will merge with one from the left. At this point stop. The track you are on bears to the right, but ahead there is an opening into what looks like a field. This opening is a road used as a public path, although it is not signposted. Take the **opening straight ahead**.

  It is easy to miss this track. Should this happen don't worry, simply follow the track to the end and you will come out at the junction encountered in the early part of the route. In this instance turn left and you soon will be back on the track used to commence this ride.

- This track goes between two fields and is fenced on each side. It's worth stopping to admire the view once or twice on this slightly downhill route. Eventually it comes out onto the gravel road where the route started.

- **Turn left** and return to the starting point.

SOUTHERN COUNTIES BIKE GUIDE

15: Knapp Down

Duration:	1 hr
Distance:	7.5 miles
Pathfinder Map:	1262
Start:	GR004267
Type of Ride:	Track and Road
Grade:	3

This route has the potential of offering some splendid views. It is mainly downhill and the initial view across Knapp Down is lovely. If the return route has been cleared then the view looking back to Knapp Down is splendid.

The route starts on the byway between the villages of Fovant and Fifield Bavant. Referring to the directions to reach Odstock village, when entering the village, instead of turning left and passing the pub, carry straight on. This road winds through the villages of

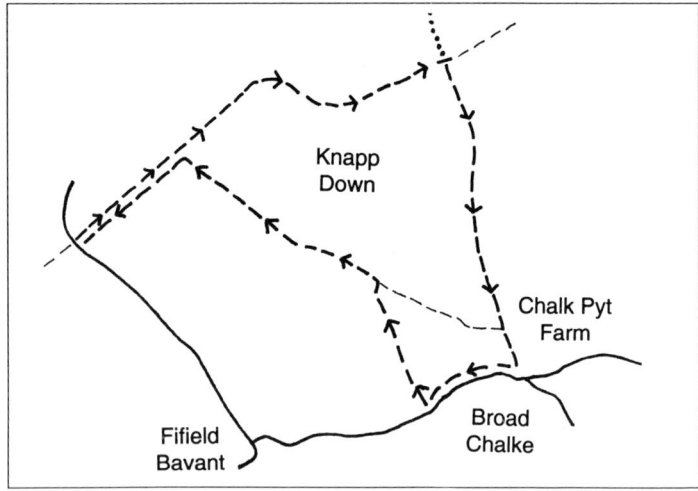

Homington and comes out into Coombe Bissett onto the A354.

At this busy junction look to your left, across the road and you will see the byway sign for the Old Blandford Road (track) which is part of the Stratford Toney route. Turn right onto the A354, as you go around the bend there is a road on your left to Stratford Toney, turn here. Follow this road through Bishopstone and when you enter Broad Chalke village keep right. Proceed through the village and come to Fifield Bavant. At this point the road will bear sharp left and there is a turning on the right. Turn right and proceed up the hill for about 1 mile. When almost at the top you will see signs for the byway marking where it crosses the main road.

- Take the **right byway** (heading east) and cycle along this track. Although on top of the down it is primarily covered with hedging so difficult to see anything. Eventually the byway opens and on the right is the spectacular view of Knapp Down.

    At this point, stop and look across the down; you should see a wooden hut in the distance, which is on the bridleway on the return route.

- Now **continue on the gravel road** which quickly changes to a track as it bears to the left. It's still easy to cycle, not hilly, but watch out for low hanging branches. This is supposed to be a byway but its a long time since a vehicle came through here. Continue along this track until you come out onto a gravel road.

- At the road **turn right**, there is a sign here stating bridle path only. There is a small reservoir nearby so you may also hear running water. Follow the very wide track to its end and don't stray off onto any of the other paths, these are private. The wide track soon turns into a road and is downhill all the way. Speeds in excess of 30 mph are possible but this is not recommended!

    The bridleway comes out at Chalk Pyt Farm in Broad Chalke village. Carefully cross the farmyard, the bridleway is straight ahead.

- Follow the road to the end and come out into Broad Chalke village. We passed this way to reach the starting point for this ride. Now **turn right** onto the road.

Knapp Down, narrow track through the woods

- **Cycle along the road**, past the houses, then see an open field on your left, pass under some telephone cables and you will see a bridleway entrance 25yds ahead on the right.

    When the author rode this route, the bridleway was virtually impassable. It is hoped that this situation has been corrected. If it has not then continue along the road until it bends sharp left. At this junction turn right and cycle up the hill to the byway entrance.

- Enter the **bridleway on the right**. It's steep and it may not be possible to cycle all of it. After what seems like an eternity you will eventually meet another track with routes to your left and right. **Turn left**.

- This track is well used by the farmer and affords some interesting views across the downs. Cycle along here until it opens out onto a gravel road. At this point you will see the wooden hut that was pointed out earlier on the byway. **Turn right**. There should be some bridleway signs here.

- Follow this track to the **gate at the end**. It's slightly hilly but I think this is a better route than the road. It's also pleasant and you are likely so see pheasants and rabbits.

- At the gate, will find an **opening on the left**. Go through here and after about 25yds you will be back at the byway. **Turn left** and you will shortly be back at the starting point.

New Forest

The New Forest probably requires no introduction to readers who enjoy our countryside. One might think that this is the perfect place to ride a mountain bike, but think again!

Recently the Forestry Commission have introduced strict guidelines with respect to mountain bikes. This is because a number of bikers have ridden without regard for the countryside. Now you may only ride along the tracks and not over the heath land. Therefore the routes described here are in the New Forest area but are not necessarily in the actual New Forest.

A good reference map is the Ordnance Survey Outdoor Leisure 22 for the New Forest. These maps not only show all the rights of way but include parking places, camping, picnic sites and tourist information offices.

16: Ivy Wood Area

Duration: 45 mins
Distance: 8.5 miles
Pathfinder Map: Outdoor Leisure 22
Start: GR315024
Type of Ride: Mainly tracks
Grade: 3

This is a predominantly off road route through the woods, but there is some road work required to reach it. The route is not too hilly and there is a lovely bridge to cross the river. The circular route through the woods, past the farm and then back into the woods reminds one of why people buy mountain bikes. There are a few hills to climb so it's a good exercise route.

Head for Brockenhurst and take the B3055 to Beaulieu. Along this road you will see a sign for the car park at Ivy Wood. The ride starts from here.

- Ride out of the car park and turn **left** onto the road.
- Approximately 100yds on the left there is a road, **turn left here**. Follow this road to the end, coming out by Brockenhurst Railway Station.
- When you come out on the road, **almost immediately turn left** and take the road which passes the church.
- This road proceeds for some distance. It bears around to the right. At the end of the road **turn left** onto the A337 and continue along the road out of Brockenhurst until it opens wide and reaches a junction.
- At this junction on the left is a road marked "No Through Road". **Take this road** and **bear right at the bend** which leads to the bridleway.
- Proceed **straight** onto the bridleway. There is a sign here denoting that the road is private for vehicles and access is for

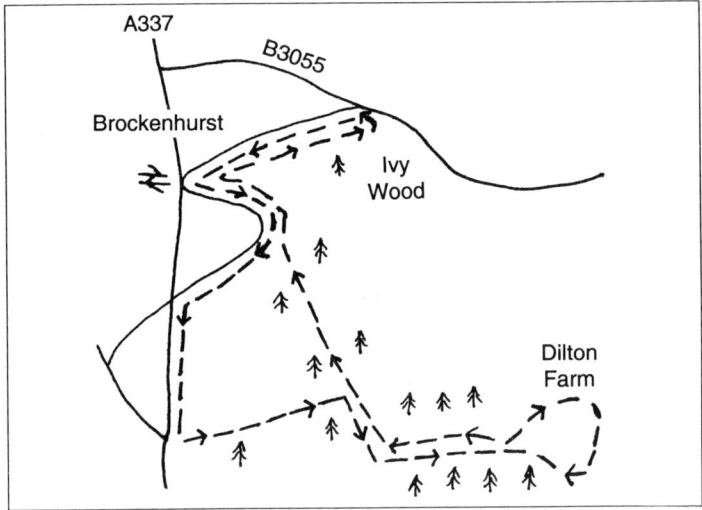

bridleway only. Enjoy cycling over the cattle grid.

This is a long gravel track, predominantly uphill, which enters into a wildlife reserve. Don't deviate onto any of the tracks on either side of this bridleway, they are private.

- Eventually the track opens and there is a track on your left. At this point **bear right**. You will know this is the correct path because it goes downhill and shortly comes to a track on the left and a gate.
- **Turn left** and **go through the gate**, please remember to close it behind you. Now on a narrow track that gently goes downhill, you soon bear around to the right, where it comes to a ford.
- **Cross the ford** (I suggest using the bridge unless you want to get wet!)
- **Cycle up the hill** (great if it's been raining) until you come to an opening and bridleway signposts pointing straight ahead and to the right. Take care cycling up this track, it can be slippery and eroded if its been raining recently.
- At the bridleway sign **turn right**. You are now on a circular route that will return to this point. This route goes through the wood, ultimately passes a house on your left and then comes out onto a road.
- There is no sign here, but **turn left** onto the bridleway. The track passes between two fields and leads to Dilton Farm. Just before the farm entrance there is a bridleway sign on the left.
- **Turn left** onto the bridleway which passes around the farm buildings and comes out onto another track. At this point the farm will be on your right. There is another track straight ahead, **turn left** here onto the gravel road.
- Follow the road until you **come to a gate** ahead. Go through the gate, remembering to close it behind you and enter the wildlife reserve.
- Continue along this track. It's narrow but fun, watch out for over-hanging nettles and prickly bushes. Eventually come out at the junction with the bridleway sign where we started this circular route. Cycle **straight ahead** to the ford.
- Return **back through the ford** onto the path and **turn right at**

the gate.

- At the wide opening where the track bears to the left and there are signs for the bridleway pointing in three directions (remember this is the route we came along at the beginning), take the path **on the right** this time. Follow this hilly climb to the end which will take about 10 minutes.
- **Go through the double gates**, then turn right onto the road that we rode along earlier. Follow this road to the end passing a church on the left.
- At the road **turn right onto the main road** and then immediately **turn right** again onto the B3055.
- Follow the B3055 to the end, **turn right, then right again** back into Ivy Wood.

17: Ashley Heath

Duration:	30 mins
Distance:	4.25 miles
Pathfinder Map:	Outdoor Leisure Map 22
Start:	GR129058
Type of Ride:	Gravel tracks
Grade:	4

This is an ideal route for beginners. There is very little road work and the tracks are all well maintained gravel paths. The route passes a golf course and goes through the Moors Valley Country Park which is an ideal place to visit after the ride because of all the amenities.

Take the B3081 off the A31 just past Ringwood. A short distance along the B3081 where the road divides there is a small parking area on the left. It is here that a bridleway goes through Ashley Heath. It may be possible to park here or further along in one of the many lay-bys. Alternatively head for the Moors Valley Country Park and start the ride from there.

NEW FOREST

- From the gate go up to the main track and **turn right**.
- Follow the track, at the first bend **bear left**. Now keep going straight ahead, passing some timber buildings which you should remember because you will need to use them as a landmark on the return journey. Look out for the blue bridleway signs to follow. This route is an easy gravel track which passes between some buildings and after about 10 minutes will come to the golf course.

    The track passes over the golf course so watch out for golf balls and don't frighten the golfers while they are swinging!

- The track comes out onto a road with buildings opposite. This is part of the Moors Valley Country Park where there are generally lots of people, dogs, cyclists and running children. **Turn left** onto the road.

    This road passes the Moors Lake and the Moors Valley Steam Railway. After the ride consider returning here to enjoy the facilities. There is a large car park and plenty of places to walk and view. Alternatively one could start the ride from here.

- Once on the road **follow the exit** signs out of the park.
- At the end of the loop road **turn left**.
- Cycle a short distance, when you reach the **Caravan Park** turn left again onto a track.
- At the **first junction** **turn left** and follow this trail.

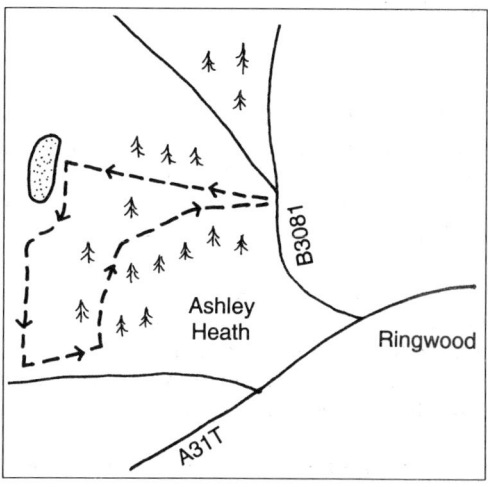

SOUTHERN COUNTIES BIKE GUIDE

- This is a **long gravel trail** with lots of walkers so take care. The park has strict rules about mountain bikes and there are signs stating where you may ride. Despite passing many trails, stay on the route until you come to a bridleway sign, where there is a junction. You will recognise the correct junction by the wooden buildings on your right that we passed at the beginning of this ride.
- Turn **right** at the junction, now back on the trail taken at the beginning.
- Cycle along this track, remembering to **turn left** to arrive back at the start point.

18: Lepe

Duration:	1hr
Distance:	9.5 miles
Pathfinder Map:	Outdoor Leisure Map 22
Start:	GR455985
Type of Ride:	Woods and roads, mud likely
Grade:	3

This is the "go to the beach" ride. Parking at Lepe beach then heading a few miles inland there is a lovely circular route through the woods which should not be too muddy. There will be quite a bit of road riding to reach the ride and to return to the car park. Then at the end of the ride, one can picnic on the beach.

Take the A326 from Southampton to Fawley. Before reaching Fawley take the turning on the right signposted to Blackfield. Follow this road to its very end which is Lepe beach and park in the car park here. Don't forget to pay the parking fee, even on Sundays! After the ride the beach is ideal for a stroll or to have a picnic.

- **Turn right** out of the car park and cycle up the road for about

12 minutes.
- Then **turn right into Walkers Road North**. Cycle to the end of the road where it changes into a track.
- **Proceed onto the track** and past the recreation ground.
- When you come out into the open you will see a footpath sign on the left, a road on the right and a gravel road ahead. **Go straight ahead**, this is Green Lane.
- At the end of this lane **turn left** and continue to a junction. The road to the left goes to the farm, **take the one to the right**.
- You will come to a gate on the left-hand side. Go **through here** and this is a great track.
- It's quite long and eventually comes out at a junction with tracks on your left and right. At the end **turn left** on to another bridleway.

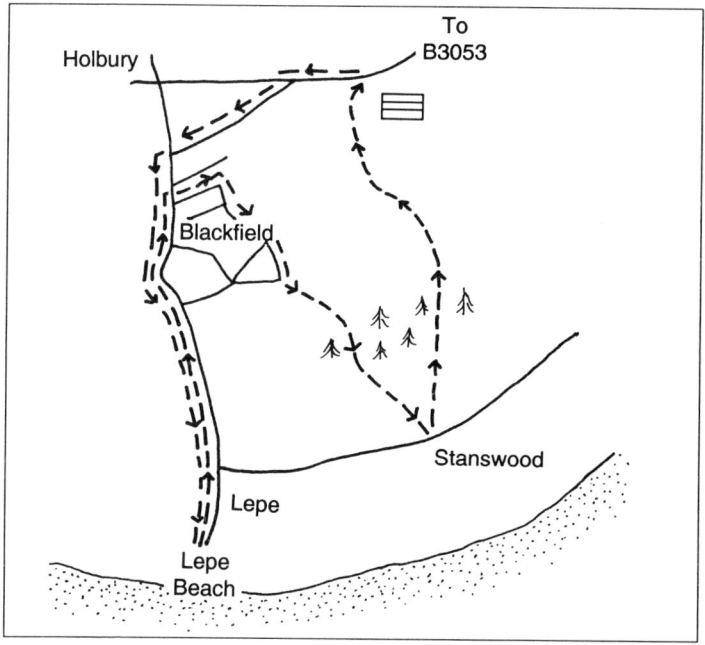

- Onward now, **up and down the hills**. This ride through the wood is rather pleasant. Take care not to frighten the fishermen as you cycle pass the river.
- Soon come to tracks in various directions but **keep going straight on.**
- When you reach the **junction by the pylon** take the track that is **straight ahead** but on the left. It's easy to be confused at this point because the route is not signposted well.
- Follow this route to the end where it comes to a gate. Go **through the gate** and cycle to the end of **Chapel Lane**.
- At the end of Chapel Lane **turn left** onto the main road. Almost immediately left is a road signposted to Blackfield.
- Turn **left here and left again**. Now on the road to the beach, in another 5 minutes you will be back at the car park.

19: Ringwood Forest

Duration: 30 mins
Distance: 4 miles
Pathfinder Map: Outdoor Leisure 22
Start: GR108078
Type of Ride: Gravel Tracks
Grade: 4

This is another route which is very suitable for beginners. It's a very short circular route which can easily be ridden twice over nice gravel paths. There are few hills and it's reasonably well marked.

Take the B3081 off the A31 just past Ringwood. A short distance along the B3081 it divides. Take the road which bears to the left and continue some distance along this road. Before reaching the village you will see a lay-by on the right-hand side, a Forestry Commission sign for Ringwood Forest and a bridleway sign. The ride starts here.

NEW FOREST

- Follow the **bridleway track** which is a vehicle wide track. It begins with a small hilly climb, but don't worry, it's the only hill.
- As you reach the top of the hill the track bears to the right and comes to a junction. A blue bridleway mark seems to indicate to bear left, but the bridleway is **straight on**. Don't take the tracks on either the left or right.
- Cycle this **track to the end** which comes out onto the road.
- **Turn left** onto the road and cycle a short distance until the road bends. **On the bend** there is a wide opening on the left. **Turn left here** and cycle towards the Forestry Commission sign.
- Be very careful here. The track straight ahead is a footpath. **Turn left** onto the bridleway, which is signposted.
- Now follow this track **back into the woods**. Don't be tempted to take any of the side tracks.
- However, when have ridden **down the hill** (be careful here, one can get up speed and there are likely to be walkers

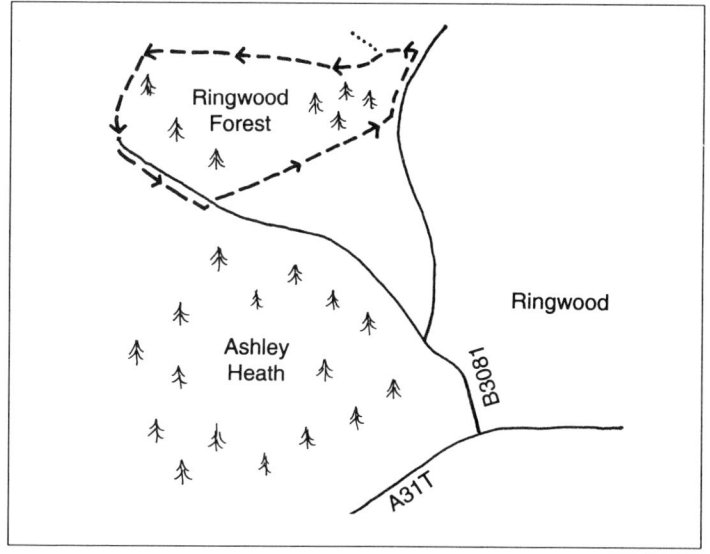

around!) come to a junction. Take the track that **bears to the right**. You should see a blue bridleway sign on the tree.

- Follow the track, keep **going straight**, under the pylons and simply follow the trail. Shortly the track reaches some houses on the left, bordered by a fence. Before the fence is an entrance and a post with a blue bridleway marker.
- **Turn left** here and ride this narrow overgrown route down to the B3081, it merges into Noon Hill Road.
- **Turn left onto the B3081** and return to your car.

This route is so short, you could almost go around for a second time.

Winchester Area

The Winchester area contains a number of bridleways which make for some good off road routes. Since this is a heavily populated area you are likely to meet people walking dogs so take care. Parking in this area is very difficult. Therefore be prepared to park your car some distance from where the routes start and cycle to the beginning.

20: Sutton Scotney

Duration:	50 minutes
Distance:	7.75 miles
Pathfinder Map:	1243
Start:	GR460339
Type of Ride:	Road and potentially muddy
Grade:	3

This is a route that is open and doesn't offer any spectacular views, except of the A34. Nevertheless it is a fairly challenging ride and will provide a pretty good workout, especially the ride home uphill on the road.

The entrance to this ride can be found by taking the A34 north to Newbury. Come off at the first junction and proceed north on the B3420. Shortly you will come to a lay-by, park here because this is one of the few suitable parking areas. This is a busy road so take care joining the road.

- From the lay-by proceed north along the B3420 until you come to sign for Pendex Oil and **turn right** here onto the bridleway, the entrance to the oil company site is on the left.

    The track is slightly hard to find, look out for signs warning of lorries turning and then you will see the opening shortly on the right. Follow this track which is about a car's width and don't deviate from the route. This path is not well marked so if at anytime you get lost, look for the horses' hoof marks.

- Cycle through **until it opens out** and there is a sort of junction here. There is a route straight ahead, a narrow track on the left and another track a little behind on the right. **Turn left** here.

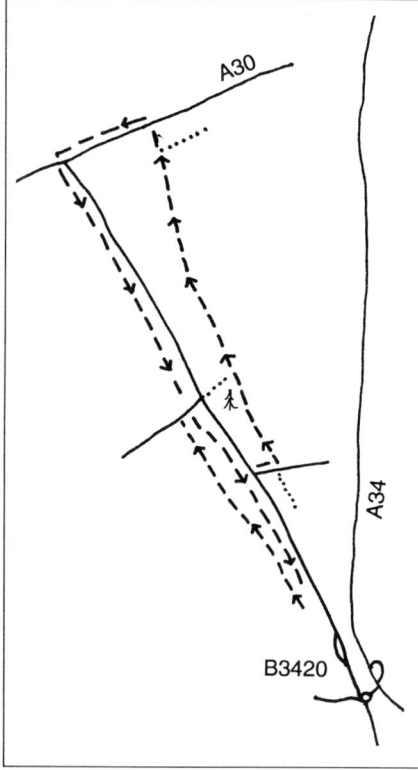

- As you proceed through the opening which could be very muddy you will see a sign on your right denoting a private route. On your left you should be able to see the oil company platform rig. **Cycle ahead** on the gravel path which is downhill all the way.

- **Follow this track to the very end**. There are points where tracks appear on the left and right but always ignore these. Stop only to admire the view or for horses which you are likely to meet on this route.

- At the end of this track you will come out onto the A30. **Turn left onto the road.**

WINCHESTER AREA

Take extra care: the A30 is very busy road and some people seem to forget that our roads have speed limits.

- Cycle along the A30 and **turn left** at the next junction onto the B3420. Now follow this road back to the lay-by where the route started.

21: Compton Down

Duration:	50 minutes
Distance:	6 miles
Pathfinder Map:	1264
Start:	GR452270
Type of Ride:	Tracks
Grade:	3

This is one of those routes that will take you by surprise. It's a great track ride only a mile or so from a motorway. The only problem is parking a short distance from the start of the route. It is also not very well signposted, but since it is gravel the route is fairly easy to find.

Parking close to this ride is rather difficult. I suggest leaving Winchester on the A3090 heading to Hursley village. Past South Winchester Golf Club on the left just past the top of the hill, approximately 100yds on the left, is a large lay-by, park here.

To start the ride cycle back up the hill, sorry, and turn right into Millers Lane which passes by the golf course. At the end of this road, the ride begins.

- Immediately opposite is a **small uphill road** advising no vehicle access. Cycle to the top and **bear right** following the track. There is no bridleway sign.
- This is a narrow path, very popular with walkers. Follow it until it turns sharply left. You then will see a **narrow path ahead** through the trees, take this uphill route which emerges

at Yew Hill.

- At Yew Hill, **turn left**, cycle the short distance to the gate and **turn right** onto a wide stony track. Now it's downhill all the way for about 15 minutes. This route has few landmarks, it's a very pleasant track between the fields. Don't be tempted to deviate onto any of the other tracks, they are private. Eventually come out at Upper Silkstead farm.

- Look carefully, on the left is a blue bridleway sign, **turn left** here which reveals a very wide track which after a very short distance **turns left again** onto another wide gravel track.

- Now **follow this wide track**, watch out for walkers. You will pass a footpath sign on your right, ignore this.

- After some distance, the track bears to the right and there is a track ahead. The route on the right is another bridleway, but we won't take that one today, instead go **straight ahead**.

- Now pass alongside a field. A little further on, the track bears to the left where there is a gate. Straight ahead, the track goes

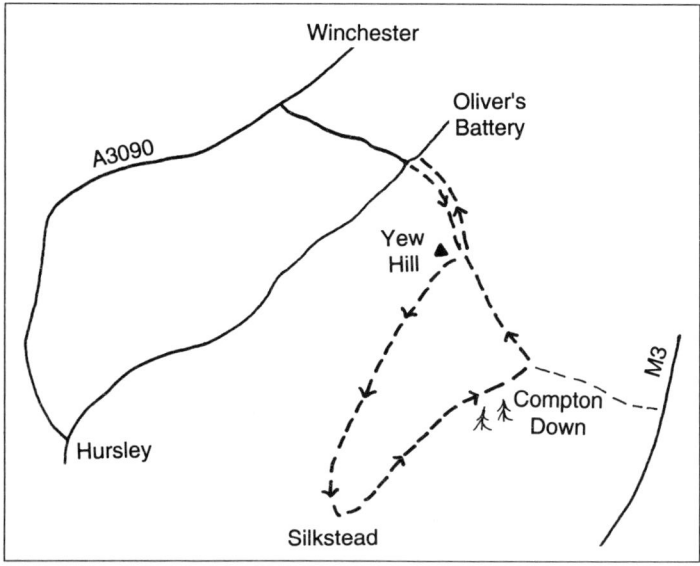

into the woods and there is a sign on the tree warning the area is private. The track with the gate is private, so proceed **straight ahead** for the woods.

This is another popular place for walkers, so take care. Follow this route to the end. Don't worry that there are no landmarks, just keep going.

- At the end come out onto another gravel track, where there is a bridleway sign. **Turn left** and proceed until you return to Yew Hill.

- At Yew Hill, return along the previous route. That is, **through the gate**, up the hill and **right onto the track**. At the end of the track **turn left** and follow the route until you reach the entrance.

- Now it is down the hill. At the bottom, **straight ahead** is Millers Lane. Take the lane, at the end, turn left and back to the lay-by where your car is parked.

Cheesefoot Head

This is a very popular area with walkers and horse riders, which is probably due to the South Downs Way crossing this area. Please make sure that you park in one of the designated car parks.

Cheesefoot Head is on the eastern side of Winchester. Take the A31 to Alton from the M3 motorway. The road begins as a ordinary road and then changes into a dual carriageway. On the opposite side of the road is the A272 to Petersfield. The entrance is found by proceeding to the roundabout and then returning in the opposite direction to the A272. Follow this road for about 1 mile, at the top of the hill there is a car park on both the left- and right-hand side.

There are many routes available from this starting point, described here are but two of many possible combinations.

22: Longwood Warren

Duration: 45 minutes
Distance: 5.25 miles
Pathfinder Map: 1264
Start: GR530276
Type of Ride: Tracks and some mud
Grade: 4

The views across the downs here are splendid. This route is a nice mixture of trails and a small amount of road work. There is only one very hilly climb and the route is well signposted.

Start at the car park on the bend which has the restricted height entrance.

CHEESEFOOT HEAD

- Proceed **through the gate**, please close it behind you and follow the bridleway track that is straight ahead. The track is a tractor's width and is well marked between the fields. As you cycle along stop to admire the view.
- You will soon come to a junction with a bridleway track on the left, ignore this sign and carry **straight on**.
- The route continues until it opens out onto a wide track by the woods. There is another bridleway on the right, ignore this sign and cycle onto the **gravel road**.

   This is a popular area so watch out for walkers, horses and low flying model aeroplanes!

- Shortly the gravel track bears sharply left. On the right is a signpost pointing to two bridleway signs, one to the left and

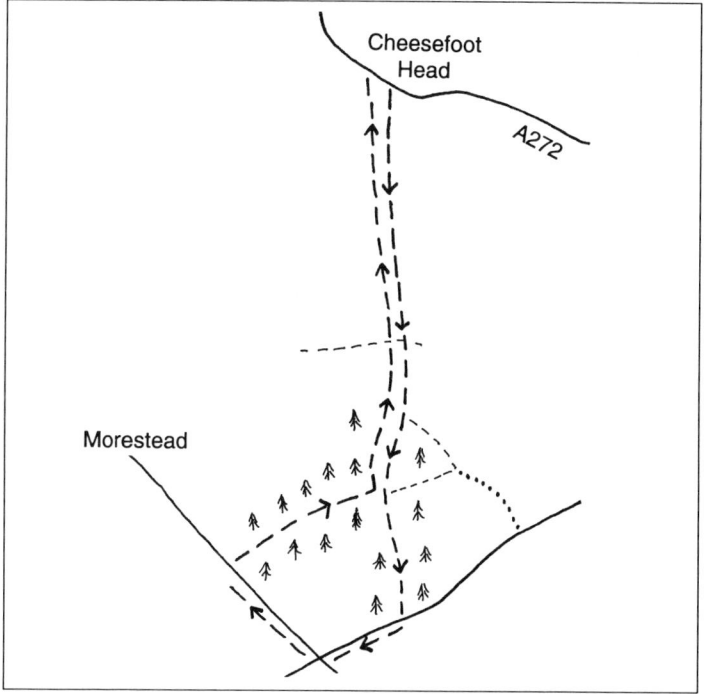

another almost straight on, into a narrow path into the woods. Take the one **straight ahead**.

- This is a long narrow track. It starts in the woods, goes downhill, then opens out at a junction of bridleways. Proceed straight ahead, making sure that you pass underneath the electricity pylons. **Follow this track until you reach the end**, where there is a gate onto the road.
- **Turn right** onto the road and cycle to the junction.
- At the junction **turn right** again. Cycle down the hill, but don't get up too much speed because the next turning is in the dip of the hill.
- In the dip of the hill there is a bridleway sign on the left, take the bridleway sign on the **right**. This is a potentially muddy route through the woods, but it is very pleasant. Don't be tempted to deviate from the track, just follow it until it comes to the junction we met previously with the bridleway signs and the electricity pylons on your right.
- **Turn left** and now cycle up the track that you previously cycled down. This track through the woods, which makes a nice hilly climb, eventually emerges onto a gravel road. Notice the bridleway signs on the left.
- Proceed **straight ahead** onto the gravel road and now back on the route used at the start of the ride. Follow the track to its end, where you will be back at the car park. The only problem with the return journey is that most of it is uphill!

23: Fawley Down

Duration:	1 hr
Distance:	6.25 miles
Pathfinder Map:	1264
Start:	GR530276
Type of Ride:	Mainly tracks
Grade:	2

There are some splendid views on this ride and most of it is in the woods. It is fairly well marked and requires minimal road work. Some of the best views are on the final route home, which in summer could be a beautiful field of yellow.

Start at the car park on the bend which has the restricted height entrance.

- Proceed **through the gate**, please close it behind you and follow the bridleway track that is straight ahead. The track is a tractor's width and is well marked between the fields. As you cycle along stop to admire the view.

- Soon you will come to a junction where there is a bridleway

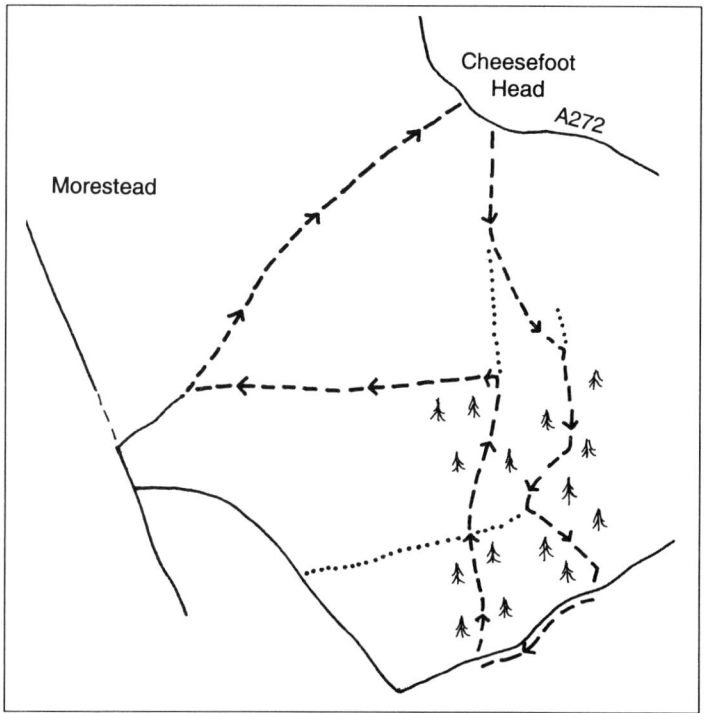

gn pointing ahead and to the **left**. Take the route to the left which is a route downhill between two fields. When the **route bears to the right, follow the track**, don't be tempted to select another path.

- Continue along the path until you come to a junction with signs pointing in various directions. Here, **bear right** onto a wide track. The track is now very wide and slightly rutted due to tractor usage.

    Locating the next part of the route is slightly difficult so take care, otherwise you could find yourself on private land. The track opens out near some electricity pylons on your left, there is a small blue bridleway marker on a post, pointing to the left and into the woods.

- **Enter the wood** as shown by the bridleway marker. The route will probably be muddy and there should be lots of horses' hoof marks.

- Follow this track, which eventually comes out onto a gravel road, **turn right** here.

- Cycle the gravel road to the junction. Once again there are signs pointing in several directions. The electricity pylon is on your right, take the **track on the left**.

- Follow the gravel **road to the end** where there is a gate onto the road. When passing through the gate please remember to close it behind you.

- Turn **right** onto the road.

    Finding the next bridleway entrance could pose a little problem if you cycle too fast along the road. About one mile along this road on the right-hand side is the next bridleway. It is located at the point where there are two large fields on either side of the road. The one on the left is open, on the right, there is a gate into the field and by the side of it a gate onto the bridleway. (This is part of the route described in the Longwood Warren route.)

- The bridleway is a wide track that goes through the woods and downhill. Just as you pass underneath the electricity pylon come to the junction met on the Longwood Warren ride. **Take the route ahead**.

- This track through the woods is uphill, stony and may be slightly rutted. Take care because the stones can easily change your direction!
- At the end of the track, it opens onto a gravel road, where there are bridleway signs pointing left, ahead and backwards. Take the **route straight ahead**.

    Here you are likely to see felled trees and smell the beautiful scent of timber.
- The track passes next to a small wood on the left. At the end of the wood, the track goes straight ahead, however if you look carefully on the left you will see a bridleway sign pointing to the left. If it has been raining this area is likely to be very muddy. **Turn left** and as you cross the mud, the bridleway starts by passing through the gate.
- Pass through the gate and **follow the track straight ahead** into the woods. This is a fun narrow track which is long and not too hilly. At one point the track opens out and there is a track on the right. Ignore the right-hand track and always carry straight on. Please follow the gravel track which eventually heads towards some houses on the left.
- At the house, turn **sharp right** onto the next bridleway. It's not signposted.
- Now follow this **track to the very end**. Initially it starts as a gravel road, which passes by the MOD range. Then it passes through a farmer's field which, depending on what has been planted, can be a beautiful field of yellow.
- From here you will be able to see the road ahead. At the end of the farmer's field, come to a junction with signs pointing ahead, left and right. **Take the one ahead** which leads in a very short distance to the road.
- Pass through the gate and **turn right** onto the road. The car park where you started is but a short distance on the left.

Other Routes

The routes in this section are in the other parts of Hampshire or in the south of Berkshire. One could be excused for thinking that a town like Reading is a busy metropolis and offers the mountain bike rider little opportunity for off road riding. If this is your opinion then try these routes, your views will surely change.

The local authority in Berkshire should be congratulated for their extensive maintenance of the route which has been called the A33 route because it runs parallel to the A33 road. If it wasn't for the noise of the traffic, you would never know that you were cycling less than a few yards from a very busy main road.

24: Along the A33

Duration: 1hr 10 mins
Distance: 6 miles
Pathfinder Map: Pathfinder 1188
Start: GR704659
Type of Ride: Mainly tracks, return via road
Grade: 3

Of all the routes in this guide book, this is the one that will probably surprise one the most. It's hard to believe that such a delightful off-road track is but a few yards from a very busy main road. Although it can be very muddy in places, it's worth it. Just be very careful when cycling along the main road.

The A33 is the main road from Basingstoke to Reading. A few miles before Reading the road changes into a dual-carriageway. On either

OTHER ROUTES

side of this road there is a bridleway which this route covers. It's an easy, fun route, and it is probably only muddy in a couple of places.

Parking for this route is a little difficult. Take the A33 north from Basingstoke, on the dual carriageway just before Reading there are lay-bys either before or after the second bridge that crosses the dual carriageway: probably best to park in the second of these lay-bys. The problem arises that you will then have to walk back to reach the start of the ride. This is a very busy road so it might be safer to park in the last lay-by and cycle to the end of the dual carriageway and then use the route as described from the roundabout to reach the start of the route. Upon completion of the route then turn left onto the main road and return to the lay-by.

- As you proceed north along the A33 towards Reading you will pass under a bridge on the dual carriageway. Shortly past the bridge on the left-hand side is a road. The route begins here. On the **left** is the track for the bridleway.

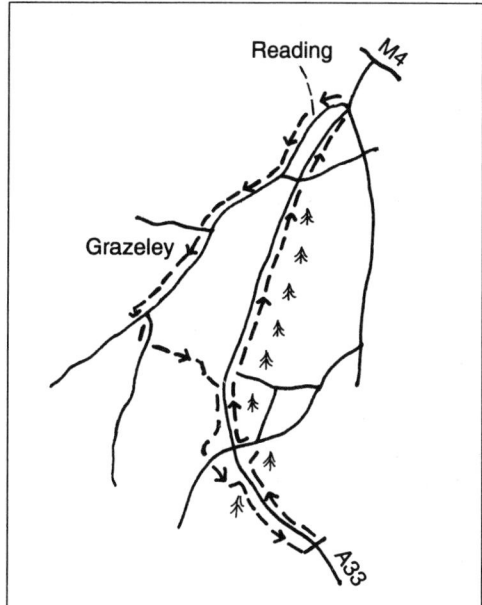

- Follow the path and **bear around to the right** where it follows the stream.
- Stay on the gravel path and don't be tempted to deviate onto any of the other paths. Just before the end the path turns sharply right and there is a bridge. You will have to dismount here to get over the board at the entrance to the bridge. This will bring one out onto the road, **turn left** onto the road.

- Cycle along the road which turns into a track and becomes the bridleway again, back to where one can see the A33. The bridleway then drops down, **turn left** to cycle underneath the bridge and then **turn left** again up a path, now on the other side of the A33.
- Enjoy cycling along this path which is adjacent to the A33. The local authority have split this route into two paths, the one on the right is for pedestrians, take **the left one** which is the bridleway. If it has been raining this route which is well used by horses, is likely to be very, very muddy.
- Follow the route through the woods, it is long so enjoy it. Eventually it comes out on the road by some private houses.
- Turn **left** onto the road and cycle a short distance, stopping just before the bridge which crosses the A33. On the **right** is the continuation of the bridleway. Follow this track again.
- Follow the track which runs alongside the A33. At the end **cross the road** and follow the track into the woods.
- This track goes back into the potentially muddy woods. When riding this route it is hard to believe sometimes that one is only a few yards from the busy A33. When you **come to the gate**, go through and close it behind you.
- Now on the road with a pond on the left, look out for the ducks in their little house. **Take the route by the pond**.
- Follow the grass track, which starts out wide and then narrows, to its very end.
- The track comes out at the roundabout at the end of the A33. **Turn left** and at the roundabout go straight across. It might be safer at this point to dismount from the bicycle and cross the A33 as a pedestrian.
- The road is signposted to Grazeley. Cycle into Grazeley village and take the **first turning left** past the school. Cycle a short distance and then **turn left** again to return to the A33 where the route started.

OTHER ROUTES

25: Stubbington Down

Duration:	45 mins
Distance:	5.5 miles
Pathfinder Map:	1203
Start:	GR516565
Type of Ride:	Hilly tracks, return via road
Grade:	2

One might wonder why this route is considered difficult. It starts off as a splendid narrow track, then there is a small amount of road work before more delightful off road tracks. Then there is the marvellous ride between the two fields before returning to the narrow tracks again. What is difficult is the ride home to one of the highest spots in Hampshire. The author made it to the top without stopping, can you?

Take the A34 North and approximately 20 miles north of Winchester take the B3400 in the direction of Whitchurch. Pass through the village of Whitchurch and head towards the village of Overton. Once in Overton turn left onto the B3051. Now stay on this road and eventually climb up a hill where there are lay-bys on the left and right. At the top of the hill is White Hill car park. Here one can either park in the lay-by or turn right into another car park which is slightly set back off the road and is up a small gravel track. This route starts from this point.

- As you cycle out of the car park, at the bottom of the slight incline, there is a route on the left marked with a sign. **Turn left** onto this route which is narrow and winds between the hedgerows.

- Soon the route opens out and there are fields around you. You should see a footpath on the left and an opening on the right. Ignore these and **proceed straight on**. The track runs along the edge of the farmer's field.

    The view here across the downs is beautiful and worth a

brief stop. Not that an excuse to stop is needed, unless you are very fit the hilly climb will necessitate a stop or two.

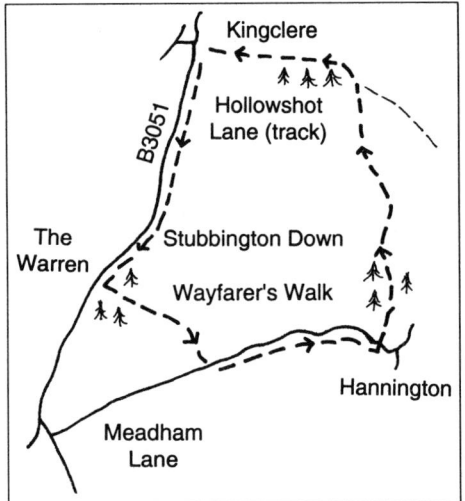

- At the top of the climb there is a gate ahead. **Proceed through the gate** remembering to close it behind you. Now follow this track to where it comes out onto the road. Enjoy this route: it has a slight incline and is a pleasure to cycle after the previous hilly route. You have just cycled another part of the Wayfarers Way.

- At the road **turn left** onto Medham Lane. Another route is signposted just ahead on the right, ignore this. Instead follow the road passing underneath some electricity pylons. At the **bend bear right** where you should see a footpath sign. Go underneath the pylons for a second time. As you start to cycle downhill you will see a bridleway sign on the left and a gate.

- **Turn left** onto this bridleway, please close the gate behind you. Now **follow the track** which bends around slightly. This is well used by horses so if unsure just look out for horses' hoof marks.

  This track runs along the side of the fields and it is very pleasant downhill and not so much fun on the uphill stretches.

- When you reach the **water tank**, the track opens out ahead and there are openings on the left and right. **Proceed straight ahead** here and follow the track around; it then passes between two fields.

OTHER ROUTES

- Eventually the track comes to an end where you will have to stop and lift the bike over a board. There are routes on the left and right. **Turn left here** but take care.
- Only a **few yards ahead on the left** is a narrow track, turn left here onto the bridleway. This route is narrow, overgrown and downhill, enjoy. But take care, it's a favourite spot for horse riders. Eventually the route opens out, changes into a road and there are houses. **Continue on until the end of the road.**
- At the end of the road **turn left**. Now you have to cycle uphill to the car park where the route started. This is very hilly and steep, but if the bike is put into first gear one can make it to the top without stopping, the author did.

26: Watership Down

Duration: 1hr 15min
Distance: 6.75 miles
Pathfinder Map: Pathfinder 1203
Start: GR516565
Type of Ride: Hilly tracks
Grade: 1

Cycling this route which has some road work and then what seems like a long uphill ride in the woods may beg the question is it "worthwhile"? It's excellent exercise and worth every penny when Watership Down is reached and you get the opportunity to cycle by the gallops. Now the question is, will any winners pass you by.

At the top of the hill is White Hill car park. Here one can either park in the lay-by or turn into another car park which is slightly set back off the road and is up a small gravel track. The route starts from this point.

- As you cycle out of the car park, at the bottom of the slight incline, there is a route on the left marked with a sign. **Turn left** onto this route which is narrow and winds between the hedgerow.

- Soon the route opens out and there are fields around. You should see a footpath on the left and an opening on the right. Ignore these and **proceed straight on**. You should see a track which is very close to the edge of the farmer's field.

  The view from here across the downs is beautiful and worth a brief stop. Not that an excuse to stop is needed, unless very fit the hilly climb will necessitate a stop or two.

- When at the top of the climb there is a gate ahead. **Proceed through the gate** remembering to close it behind you. Now follow this track to where it comes out onto the road. Enjoy this route; it has a slight incline and is a pleasure to cycle after the previous hilly route. You have just cycled another part of the Wayfarers Way.

- **Turn right** onto the road. It's worth trying to gain some speed on the downhill stretch to avoid a hard uphill ride. Proceed to the end of the road.

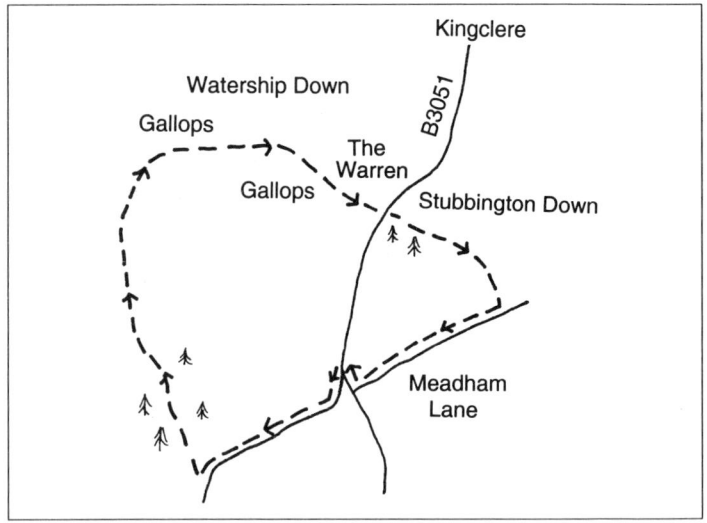

OTHER ROUTES

Author on downhill leg of Watership Down route

- At the end of the road **turn right** and cycle the short distance to the end of this road then **turn left**.
- **Proceed along this road** which is hilly. A few stops may be required. Eventually the road bears sharp left at the top of the hill. As you come around the bend you will see the downhill run but don't get carried away because the next part of the route is a few yards ahead on the right-hand side.
- **On the right** is an opening which appears to be going back almost in the same direction that we have just travelled, take this route. Proceed along this track which is quite a hilly climb.
- Follow this track uphill until it opens out onto a gravel track. You will see a road on your left and right, the one on the right heads to the farm. Ignore these routes and go **straight ahead onto the grassy route**. There is no sign here but if you look a fair way ahead will see a wooden sign in the distance.
- When the wooden sign is reached there is a gate, **go through**, closing it behind you, onto another track.

- At the **next gate go through again**, but at this point the track will narrow considerably.

  By this time you are probably thinking that have done nothing else but ride uphill on this route. However at this moment you will feel sure that the effort has been worth it because the view of the gallops at the top of the down is splendid.

- Immediately ahead you should see the gallops. Watch out for fast moving horses here. **Bear to the right** and I suggest stick well over to the right-hand side. Take care here, don't stray too far to the right because part of this area is private and it should be signposted.

- Enjoy cycling alongside the gallops, eventually you will come out onto a gravel road. Now it's downhill all the way back to the car park.

This route is very busy with walkers and horse riders so please take great care and be prepared to slow down and dismount if necessary.

27: Queen Elizabeth Forest

Duration: 45 minutes
Distance: 7 miles
Pathfinder Map: 1285
Start: GR734198
Type of Ride: Track and road
Grade: 1

This route is a little different because part of it uses a special track designed for mountain bike riders. However, in my opinion the kind creators of this track did not have novice mountain bike riders in mind. Therefore one might like to give it a miss until slightly proficient. Alternatively, be prepared to dismount and walk in places. Don't be a hero, you might live

OTHER ROUTES

to regret it! There are also plenty of signs on this route requesting mountain bike riders to keep to the designated tracks, please abide by them.

Leave Portsmouth and head north on the A3(M). Just past Horndean take the exit for Chalton and drive into Chalton village. Upon entering the village, the road bears to the right and there is a turning on the left before the church just before the telephone box. Turn left and continue along this road, as it bears to the right and goes downhill, there is a junction on the left, turn left here. You will know if you have missed the turning because the road will turn sharply left. Follow this narrow road known as Newbarn Road for several miles. It eventually comes to a junction and the Forestry Commission car park for Halls Hill is on the left. The ride starts here.

This route can be ridden in reverse direction if the prospect of a hard hill climb at the beginning is a bit daunting.

- Start the route by **reading the signs about mountain bikes**, then enter the Forestry Commission land and **cycle up the hill**. It's rather steep, so if you must stop, choose a spot where there is a bench and you can admire the view.

- The gravel track eventually opens out into a wide area where a route joins from the right. Proceed **straight ahead keeping to the left** following the blue bridleway signs.

- After a short distance, you will see **on the right the designated mountain bike**

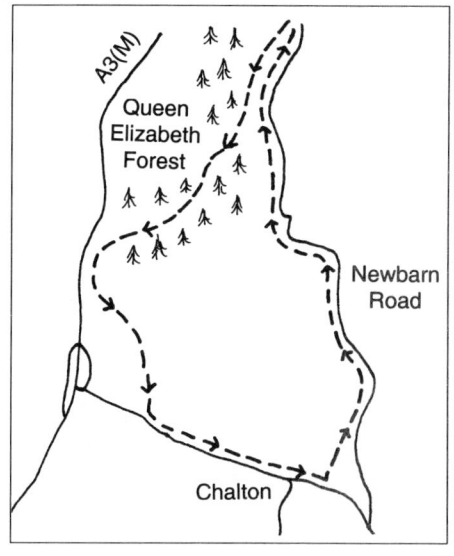

track. It's marked by posts with a yellow top and bicycle. Enjoy this great route which will challenge most "weekend" bike riders because it is hilly, very steep in places and narrow.

Please keep to the track and don't deviate from it. One can have enough fun staying on the route. One tip though, watch out for other bike riders coming in both directions. There is little point in trying to describe the route, simply follow the markers to the end.

The route comes out at Gravel Hill car park which is part of Queen Elizabeth Country Park. Alternatively one could start the route from here.

- Cycle out of the car park, **turn left** and follow the road. You will see a private sign on the left and just ahead of this on the left is the blue sign denoting the entrance to the bridleway. **Turn left onto the bridleway**.

- The bridleway is short and adjacent to a large green area. After approximately 100yds come to a **bridleway roundabout**, where there is a track to the left and one that bears right signposted to Chalton.

- **Bear right**, the track initially is close to the A3(M) then it heads away and up and offers a good view of the surrounding area. This gravel track is undulating and if there is stock car racing in the adjacent field, its a good place to stop for a moment and watch the cars. Follow the bridleway until it comes out on the road.

   This is the road into Chalton village that you came along previously to find the start of the route.

- At the road **turn left** and cycle into Chalton village, **turning left** as described just before the telephone box, the road is signposted to Compton.

- Approximately 200yds on the left, just past the farm buildings on the right is a byway entrance which is not signposted. **Turn left** onto the byway following it to completion, taking care at the end section which is downhill.

- At the end of the byway **turn left** and now back on Newbarn Road. Follow this road to the car park where the route started.

OTHER ROUTES

28: Stansted Forest

Duration:	50 minutes
Distance:	7 miles
Pathfinder Map:	1285
Start:	GR754100
Type of Ride:	Tracks, road and some mud
Grade:	3

This route has the honour of being able to shake parts in your body that you never knew existed! It's a strange route because although most of it is bridleway, the bridleway is actually a road so it's ideal for beginners and is fairly well signposted. A nice combination of gravel and dirt tracks with some mud, it has something for everyone.

Take the A3(M) North from Winchester and leave at the sign for the B2149 for Rowlands Castle. As you leave the A3(M), turn right at the end of the slip road, cross the A3(M) and at the small roundabout turn left. A short distance along this road turn right onto Rowlands Castle Road. Follow this road to the end which comes out at the village of Finchdean and you should see a public house on the left. Turn right onto Dean Lane which shortly passes under a railway bridge and comes out at a junction. Turn left, passing a few houses and turn right at the next opportunity. This is the road where the route begins, park in one of the lay-bys along this road on the right-hand side.

This route is a mixture of off road and road and you are likely to see quite a lot of wildlife including rabbits, peacocks, hens and pheasants.

- Leave the lay-by and **turn right** onto the road. Proceed down to the bend where you will see the Stansted Sawmills on the right. Look carefully and you will see a small bridleway sign on the left. This route is fairly well marked with wooden signs which are often rather faded and weathered.

SOUTHERN COUNTIES BIKE GUIDE

- **Turn left** onto the bridleway. There are likely to be piles of wood on either side, proceed straight ahead and into a field. As one enters the field it is likely to be difficult to detect the bridleway, but look ahead and in the left-hand corner you will see one sign, then another in the right-hand corner of the field. Follow the signs up to the road.

- The road is a bridleway with signs asking horse riders to stay within 2 metres of the road edge. **Proceed ahead** on the road.

  As you go along the road you will see signs for a bridleway and footpath on the left. Ignore these and proceed ahead to the white gate which is marked private.

- Just before the white gate there should be a bridleway sign

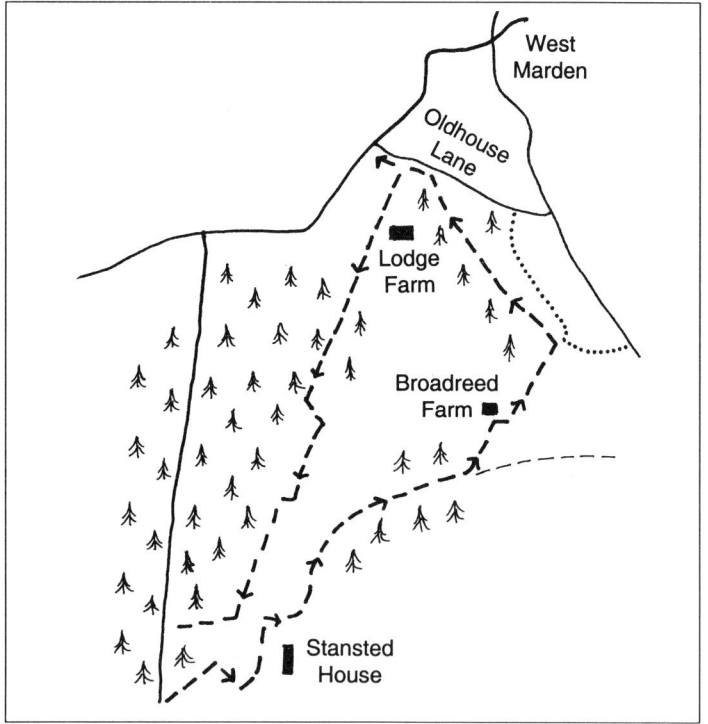

indicating the path **to the left** which goes in front of the house. Stop for a moment to admire Stansted House.

- At the end of this short track you are once again back on the road. Stop for a moment here and look to the left. You may just be able to see a gate to the right. This is where the route will return. **Turn right** onto the road and **bear left** at the bend ignoring the entrance to Stansted House.

  Now stay on the road for a considerable period of time. Pass Lumley Seat House, a property in the woods, then another cottage on the left before coming to Broadreed Farm.

- Just before the farm entrance there is a footpath and bridleway sign. **Turn right** onto the bridleway which is a gravel road. Now follow this gravel road which first bears to the left, then bears right before passing between some fields. You will then come to another house on the left and immediately ahead there should be a bridleway sign. **Turn left** here.

- Cycle a very short distance into the woods. Look very carefully for another bridleway sign where there are tracks going left, right and straight ahead. **Take the left** track which is a narrow track into the woods.

  Until this point the route could be considered quite easy, but now the fun starts because this track is designed for horses and obstacles have been placed across the route for them to jump. Therefore some dismounting of the bicycle may be required. In addition it could be very muddy.

- Nevertheless enjoy this route through the woods and follow it to the end where it comes out onto the road. **Turn left** onto the road and cycle a short distance up a small incline where you should see a bridleway sign on the left and a footpath on the right.

- The bridleway entrance is blocked by a gate but there is a small entrance on the right of the gate. **Turn left** onto the bridleway.

- Follow this track which comes out by some farm buildings and a tarmac road on the right. At this point the signs may be a little confusing. **Turn left** onto the road and pass the farm buildings. There is likely to be an open gate which says private road but the private road is a short distance along on the left. Follow the road to the field where you should see another bridleway sign which points **across the middle of the field**. This is a well used track so look out for horses' hoof marks.

- After crossing the field come to the woods and you will see another bridleway sign. Follow the route **straight into the woods** which is great fun. Once again this part of the route could be muddy.

- Eventually come to another bridleway sign on the left. **Bear left** here and follow the signs around so that route comes out on the edge of a field. Follow this bone shaking route downhill to the end. This part of the route will shake loose anything, you have been warned, my front mudguard almost came off.

- At the end of the track come out at the gate described earlier just in front of Stansted House. **Turn right** onto the road and return to the road where the ride started.

Appendix

Duration

Duration hrs:mins	Route No.	Description	Distance miles	Map	Grade	Mud
00:25	1	Itchen Wood	2.5	Pathfinder 1243	4	Yes
00:30	17	Ashley heath	4.25	Outdoor Leisure 22	4	No
	19	Ringwood Forest	4	Outdoor Leisure 22	4	No
00:45	22	Longwood Warren	5.25	Pathfinder 1264	4	Yes
	25	Stubbington Down	5.5	Pathfinder 1203	2	No
	5	Closedown Wood	6	Pathfinder 1224	3	Yes
	27	Queen Elizabeth Forest	7	Pathfinder 1285	1	Yes
	2	Around Northington	7	Pathfinder 1243	4	No
	16	Ivy Wood	8.5	Outdoor Leisure 22	3	Yes
00:50	21	Compton Down	6	Pathfinder 1264	3	No
	14	Whitsbury Down	6.25	Pathfinder 1262	4	No
	10	Yarmouth	6.75	Outdoor Leisure 29	3	No
	28	Stansted Forest	7	Pathfinder 1285	3	No
	20	Sutton Scotney	7.75	Pathfinder 1243	3	Yes
00:55	9	Four Marks	5.75	Pathfinder 1244	3	Yes
	3	Itchen Stoke Down	6	Pathfinder 1243	3	No
	8	Ox Drove	6.25	Pathfinder 1243	3	No
	4	Abbotstone	7.25	Pathfinder 1243	3	No
01:00	23	Fawley Down	6.25	Pathfinder 1264	2	No
	7	Weston Common	6.5	Pathfinder 1224	2	Yes
	6	Weston Common Long Lane	6.5	Pathfinder 1224	2	Yes
	15	Knapp Down	7.5	Pathfinder 1262	3	No
	18	Lepe	9.5	Outdoor Leisure 22	3	Yes
01:10	24	Along the A33	6	Pathfinder 1188	3	Yes
	12	Clearbury Ring	8	Pathfinder 1262	2	No
01:15	11	Ventnor	5.5	Outdoor Leisure 29	1	No
	13	Stratford Toney	6	Pathfinder 1262	2	Yes
	26	Watership Down	6.75	Pathfinder 1203	1	No

Grade: 1 - Difficult   2 - Hard   3 - Moderate   4 - Easy

Distance

Distance miles	Route No.	Description	Duration hrs:mins	Map	Grade	Mud
2.5	1	Itchen Wood	00:25	Pathfinder 1243	4	Yes
4.5	19	Ringwood Forest	00:30	Outdoor Leisure 22	4	No
4.25	17	Ashley heath	00:30	Outdoor Leisure 22	4	No
5.25	22	Longwood Warren	00:45	Pathfinder 1264	4	Yes
5.5	25	Stubbington Down	00:45	Pathfinder 1203	2	No
	11	Ventnor	01:15	Outdoor Leisure 29	1	No
5.75	9	Four Marks	00:55	Pathfinder 1244	3	No
6	5	Closedown Wood	00:45	Pathfinder 1224	3	Yes
	21	Compton Down	00:50	Pathfinder 1264	3	No
	3	Itchen Stoke Down	00:55	Pathfinder 1243	3	No
	24	Along the A33	01:10	Pathfinder 1188	3	Yes
	13	Stratford Toney	01:15	Pathfinder 1262	2	Yes
6.25	14	Whitsbury Down	00:50	Pathfinder 1262	4	No
	8	Ox Drove	00:55	Pathfinder 1243	3	No
	23	Fawley Down	01:00	Pathfinder 1264	2	No
6.5	7	Weston Common	01:00	Pathfinder 1224	2	Yes
	6	Weston Common-Long Lane	01:00	Pathfinder 1224	2	Yes
6.75	10	Yarmouth	00:50	Outdoor Leisure 29	3	No
	26	Watership Down	01:15	Pathfinder 1203	1	No
7	27	Queen Elizabeth Forest	00:45	Pathfinder 1285	1	Yes
	2	Around Northington	00:45	Pathfinder 1243	4	No
	28	Stansted Forest	00:50	Pathfinder 1285	3	No
7.25	4	Abbotstone	00:55	Pathfinder 1243	3	No
7.5	15	Knapp Down	01:00	Pathfinder 1262	3	No
7.75	20	Sutton Scotney	00:50	Pathfinder 1243	3	Yes

Distance miles	Route No.	Description	Duration hrs:mins	Map	Grade	Mud
8	12	Clearbury Ring	01:10	Pathfinder 1262	2	No
8.5	16	Ivy Wood	00:45	Outdoor Leisure 22	3	Yes
9.5	18	Lepe	01:00	Outdoor Leisure 22	3	Yes

Grade:1 - Difficult   2 - Hard   3 - Moderate   4 - Easy

Route Difficulty

Grade	Route No.	Description	Duration hrs:mins	Distance miles	Map	Mud
1	27	Queen Elizabeth Forest	00:45	7	Pathfinder 1285	Yes
	11	Ventnor	01:15	5.5	Outdoor Leisure 29	No
	26	Watership Down	01:15	6.75	Pathfinder 1203	No
2	25	Stubbington Down	00:45	5.5	Pathfinder 1203	No
	23	Fawley Down	01:00	6.25	Pathfinder 1264	No
	6	Weston Common-Long Lane	01:00	6.5	Pathfinder 1224	Yes
	7	Weston Common	01:00	6.5	Pathfinder 1224	Yes
	12	Clearbury Ring	01:10	8	Pathfinder 1262	No
	13	Stratford Toney	01:15	6	Pathfinder 1262	Yes
3	5	Closedown Wood	00:45	6	Pathfinder 1224	Yes
	16	Ivy Wood	00:45	8.5	Outdoor Leisure 22	Yes
	21	Compton Down	00:50	6	Pathfinder 1264	No
	10	Yarmouth	00:50	6.75	Outdoor Leisure 29	No
	28	Stansted Forest	00:50	7	Pathfinder 1285	No
	20	Sutton Scotney	00:50	7.75	Pathfinder 1243	Yes
	9	Four Marks	00:55	5.75	Pathfinder 1244	No
	3	Itchen Stoke Down	00:55	6	Pathfinder 1243	No
	8	Ox Drove	00:55	6.25	Pathfinder 1243	No
	4	Abbotstone	00:55	7.25	Pathfinder 1243	No
	15	Knapp Down	01:00	7.5	Pathfinder 1262	No
	18	Lepe	01:00	9.5	Outdoor Leisure 22	Yes
	24	Along the A33	01:10	6	Pathfinder 1188	Yes
4	1	Itchen Wood	00:25	2.5	Pathfinder 1243	Yes
	17	Ashley heath	00:30	4.25	Outdoor Leisure 22	No
	19	Ringwood Forest	00:30	4	Outdoor Leisure 22	No
	22	Longwood Warren	00:45	5.25	Pathfinder 1264	Yes
	2	Around Northington	00:45	7	Pathfinder 1243	No
	14	Whitsbury Down	00:50	6.25	Pathfinder 1262	No

Grade: 1 - Difficult   2 - Hard   3 - Moderate   4 - Easy